Lille
A26

Amiens

A1

ny ✈ CDG
PARIS ●
✈ ORY
Fontainebleau

Orléans

A6   A5

Bourges

A71

aurroux

A89   A75

camadour

Figeac

dez

i   Millau

Carcassonne

ix

Reims

Verdun

Épernay   Chalons   A4

Troyes

Auxerre   Larges

Dijon

Beaune
Meursault

Mâcon

Lyon   A48

St. Étienne

Valence

Alès

Tarn
Gorge

Nîmes

Avignon

Arles

Montpellier   Carmargue

Perpignan

Luxembourg

GERMANY

Metz

Nancy   Strasbourg

Ribeauvillé

Colmar

A36

Besançon   SWITZERLAND

Geneva

L

Annecy   Chamonix

Grenoble   Torino

Gap   ITALY

Digne

N85

Aix en P   Nice
A8   Cannes

N98   St-Tropez
Marseille

Mediterranean Sea

The Essential Guide for Driving in

France

*A no-nonsense guide to the ins and outs
of driving in France*

Orv Strandoo

BOOK PUBLISHERS NETWORK

Book Publishers Network
P.O. Box 2256
Bothell • WA • 98041
Ph • 425-483-3040

10 9 8 7 6 5 4 3 2

Printed in the United States of America
LCCN: 2007932343
ISBN10: 1-887542-53-1
ISBN13: 978-1-887542-53-1

Editor: Vicki McCown
Cover Design: Laura Zugzda
Interior Layout: Stephanie Martindale

Table of Contents

REGIONAL MAPS

ODDS AND ENDS

France

I N T R O D U C T I O N

From the vast and historic beaches of Normandy to the blue waters of the Côte d'Azur, the natural beauty of France is best experienced by car. There is simply no substitute for the freedom of the open road for exploring the vineyards of Burgundy and Bordeaux, the lavender fields of Provence, or the grandeur of the Alps. With the most varied land-scape in Europe, France offers endless possibili-ties for unique travel adventures.

The suggested itineraries have been designed so that each day of driving includes the most impor-tant things to see and do. You may want to see all those things, choose only one or two, or do none at all. You could use several of these routings to cre-ate an entire trip, or select a few for traveling from point to point. You may want to travel twice as fast as the itinerary or twice as slowly. It's the routing that counts. How you go about exploring France is entirely up to you.

The quality of the overall road network is indeed impressive. Directional and informational signs are excellent, and the service areas along the autoroute are the best in Europe. State-of-the-art highway construction projects continue unabated to help transport goods, services, friendly tourists, and locals to and from every corner of the country. Even in rural areas, roads are well maintained and, for the most part, smooth.

Centuries ago, the ancient trade routes of France laid out the foundation for today's remarkable system of roads and highways. An example of this can be found in the original route between Paris and Lyon, which by the late 19th century and the advent of the automobile had become the N 4. Still a major non-toll highway, the N 4 now runs parallel to its descendant, the modern high-speed A 4 toll autoroute. **For those of you on a slower pace, you will always have the choice of traveling on a non-toll road.**

The astonishing Millau Viaduct Bridge, completed in 2004 over the River Tarn in Central France, is 1.5 miles long and soars almost 1000 feet high—taller than the Eiffel Tower, which reaches a little over 900 feet. A technological and engineering marvel, this bridge exemplifies what France and the rest of the EU are continually willing to do to improve and update their country's infrastructure.

A few years ago, French officials launched a sweeping crackdown on traffic-related deaths caused largely by excessive speed. All of a sudden speed limits and rules of the road laws became strictly enforced, and hidden cameras, radar devices, and speed traps were put into full operation. This effort has resulted in a whopping 18 percent reduction in highway fatalities, which is good news for anyone who wants to travel by car through France.

However, this stringent enforcement also means you want to abide by the traffic laws at all times. Fines are heavy and payable on the spot. If your violation is particularity serious, your vehicle will be impounded and you could land in jail. (If you've been drinking, they'll probably throw away the key.) Those caught on camera receive a written notice—complete with your car's mug shot—and an invoice for prompt payment. If you're driving a rented car, the resulting fine will be automatically added to your car hire bill. Don't forget, the rental company has your credit card on file.

If you're renting a car, unless you make an advance reservation for an automatic, chances are your car will be a stick shift. Cars with a manual transmission are preferred by locals for a couple of reasons. They get better gas mileage than automatics, important in a country where gas prices are considerably higher than they are here at home. And since cars with stick shifts are usually smaller, they give drivers a definite advantage while navigating those country roads and medieval villages.

The high-speed autoroute is most useful when you need to cover long distances to quickly reach your intended destination. It's also great for those times you want to speed through uninteresting landscapes or avoid getting stuck in possible traffic congestion around large urban centers like Toulouse, Dijon, or Marseille.

There are certain areas of the country where you'll encounter any number of tunnels, whether in the Alps or along the Riviera heading into Italy. These tunnels vary in length from as short as 150 feet along the coast to the Mt. Blanc tunnel that runs for seven miles. Even though the lighting in the tunnels is quite good, and you are required to turn on your headlights as you travel through, the tunnel still becomes darker and darker as the length increases. **If you're wearing prescription sunglasses, keep a pair of your regular glasses handy for a quick change.**

French drivers are just about the same as their European counterparts insofar as they drive fast (but not quite as fast anymore), still tailgate (but not quite as much anymore), and tend to be aggressive in crowded traffic conditions. When in doubt, be patient, go slowly, and yield to the other driver if that makes him (or her) happy.

Summing Up: The best time for travel is definitely spring or fall. Remember the rules for driving on the autoroute. Obey the speed limit—even if some drivers around you don't. Stay out of the far left lane except to pass. Never pass on the right. Use "attended" parking lots or garages when visiting city sights or major attractions. When away from your vehicle, keep maps, guidebooks, and hand-carry bags tucked out of sight. Gas up when the needle dips under a quarter tank.

But most of all, in addition to savoring *les spécialtiés gastronomiques* of the French table, enjoy discovering the many visual delights of this diverse and fascinating country. Smile, talk slowly, be polite, and who knows? You may even make a friend or two along the way.

This is a very big country, and you'll not see it all in one go, but—and you can trust me on this one—you will be back!

Bon voyage!

A Note on Maps and More...

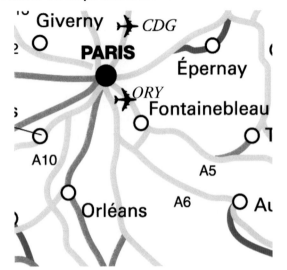

The book you're holding focuses on what you need to know to embark on a self-guided driving adventure of France. Throughout the itineraries you will find several maps to help you on your way. These maps are specifically designed to quickly acquaint you with the geography of a particular region, so they are neither detailed nor drawn exactly to scale. However, they do allow you see at a glance the general distance between towns and cities. For example, you might want to know where Antibes or Monte-Carlo is in relation to Nice or whether Beaune, in Burgundy, is closer to Dijon or Lyon. The enclosed maps give you a quick and easy reference.

Once you've made a decision on where you want to go, you will want to unfold your detailed, professional map for more information on specific route particulars and road numbers. We suggest the *Michelin* series of both national and regional maps. The applicable map number will be shown on the map page as well as in the point-to-point suggested routings.

Throughout the itinerary, we have used stars to indicate sites and locales with special appeal:

 Major importance; not to be missed
Significant site; recommended
Notable place of interest

Every effort has been made to ensure that the routings in this book are as correct and current as possible. However, each year invariably brings changes due to new road construction, improvements on existing roads, and the renumbering of various highways. Normally, any changes you may encounter will be minor and should not affect your route—but perhaps make your journey a little more exciting.

Finally—we've written this book to act as your friendly guide throughout France, providing suggested itineraries and concise descriptions of towns, villages, and important sites along the way. However, if you want more specifics other than what you'll get when you visit a particular site, then there are numerous travel books and publications in varying degrees of thickness and detail to oblige just about every taste. Pick one that suits you best.

And now, it's time to visit France!

About Those Marks Above Certain Letters...

To those of you who have studied French, kindly disregard the following.

Of all those little marks over certain letters in certain words, there is only one that you really need to know for the sake of pronunciation: that accent often seen above an "e" at the end of a word. This is the famous accent aigu (ay-goo), and what it does is turn that "é" into an "ay" sound. So "marché" (market) becomes "mar-shay," "café" (coffee) turns into "ca-fay," and "fermé" (closed) is pronounced "fair-may." Voilà! You now speak French!

France

DRIVING INFORMATION

GENERAL RULES OF THE ROAD

- Drive on the right-hand side of the road.

- On the high-speed autoroute, keep to the right and pass on the left only.

- It is illegal to pass on the right.

- Vehicles coming from the right have the right of way in cities and towns. *Priorité à droite* means you must yield to traffic coming from your right. However, traffic on main roads (indicated by a yellow diamond sign) have the right of way.

- Do not cross a solid continuous white line.

- U-turns are not permitted unless posted.

- Using a hand-held cell phone while driving is prohibited.

- Blood alcohol level is 0.5%. This is very near zero-tolerance. Penalties imposed are severe.

- Horns are to be used in emergencies only. Honking hello at a friend across the street will get you a ticket, if the police are nearby.

- Seatbelts are compulsory for the driver and all passengers. Children under 10 are not allowed in the front seat. Infants and small children require their own age-appropriate car seat.

- Pedestrians have the right of way in crosswalks.

- Traffic rules and regulations are strictly enforced as never before, and heavy fines are payable on the spot.

SPEED LIMITS

- Autoroute (*péage-toll*)
  130 kph/81 mph
  (if raining, 110 kph / 68 mph)

- Dual-Divided Highways 110 kph/81 mph
  (if raining, 100 kph / 62 mph)

- Single Highways   90 kph / 56 mph
  (if raining, 80 kph / 50 mph)

- Cities, Towns, Villages
  50 kph / 31 mph

NOTE: If driving in heavy fog, with visibility less than 50 meters / 55 yards, the speed limit will drop to 50 kph / 31 mph.

THE ROADS

- AUTOROUTES (*autoroutes à péage)* are the fast, multi-lane, toll superhighways that link the country. (In Germany, it's the autobahn, in Italy, the autostrada, etc.) Péage means toll. Autoroutes are designated by the letter A and signs are **blue**. The high-speed autoroute can be used to get you easily and quickly through areas of little interest or to get someplace in a hurry. Traveling via the autoroute can be a rather expensive affair, but the cost is usually worth it because of the time saved.

Begin autoroute   **End autoroute**

One of the most convenient aspects of auto-route driving is the presence of rest stops every 30 or 40 km. These complexes contain multi-pump gas stations, clean bathroom facilities, restaurants, coffee bars, food shops with ready made salads and sandwiches, fruit, bottled water, juice, cheese, yogurt, and lunch meats—everything needed for a picnic. Some of the smaller stops will also have picnic areas. Motel-style accommodations can be found every 100 km or so.

Pay toll at 1000 meters

- Tolls

  The autoroutes (*péage*) are subject to tolls that can be paid by cash or credit card. When entering the toll plaza, simply take a ticket from the machine. When leaving the autoroute, hand the ticket to the attendant, and the amount due will appear on the screen. **The easiest way to pay is by credit card.** The attendant swipes it and hands it right back.

Nothing to sign—takes about 10 seconds.

Pay by credit card

Take your ticket for the péage

If you find yourself in a non-attended line, just follow the ticket and credit card directions printed in English on the automatic machine. Easy.

Péage attendant cash or credit

Automatic pay with euro coins

If you find yourself on a road that turns into an autoroute, then you'll have to stop after a short distance to make a payment by either credit card or cash.

On some shorter segments of the autoroute, signs will depict coins going into a basket, so make sure to keep some euro coins handy. No bills—only coins accepted.

SAMPLE APPROXIMATE AUTOROUTE CHARGES

    Paris – Lyon €30
    Paris – Reims €10
    Paris – Tours €21
    Paris – Nice €68

DON'T FORGET THE BASIC RULES OF THE AUTOROUTE

- Drive on the right and pass on the left.
- It is strictly forbidden to pass on the right.
- The left lanes are for passing only.

    This is the law! **You cannot hang out in the left lane** like so many drivers do at home. Make your pass and get back in that right lane. Not only will you be safer there, you will also be observing the same rules as the other drivers on the road. And if you get caught just cruising in the left lane, you will be ticketed.

- NATIONAL HIGHWAY SYSTEM ROADS *(routes nationales)* are the major **non-toll** two-lane highways (although some highways may have multiple lanes or even be divided) that connect the principle cities and towns. They are designated by the letter N—and occasionally RN—on **green** signs. Before the advent of the autoroute, these roads made up the original highway system of the country.

- DEPARTMENTAL ROADS *(routes départementales)* are local government roads that link the smaller towns and villages, much like our county roads. They are designated by the letters D or C on **white** signs. Sometimes these signs will not show the road number, but simply list the names of the towns along the route.

A word of caution: Since so much of France is agricultural, slow-moving farm equipment as well as road-clogging livestock will be part of your driving experience. Slow down, enjoy the moment, and smell the roses...well, maybe that smell will actually be from something else. Just remember—the animals have the right of way!

One more word of caution: Three lane roads can still be found in some sections of the country. Beware: They can be downright dangerous. On these roads, the two outer lanes go in opposite directions, but the middle lane is used for passing in **both** directions. The danger of this "Russian Roulette" approach to traffic control is immediately evident to anyone trying to navigate French highways. If and when you encounter this traffic "faux pas," do your best to stay out of that middle lane!

International numbered signs: Found only on the autoroute, these green signs designated by the letter E are posted for the convenience of truckers and long-distance drivers going from one European country to another. Example: The E 80 green-and-white numbered sign will be displayed starting outside Lisbon, continue through Spain and France, and end in southern Italy.

International road sign designation

ROUNDABOUTS

- When approaching a roundabout, drivers must **yield to vehicles already in the roundabout**. The yield approach sign will read "*Cédez le passage*," which means to yield or give way, or "*Vous n'avez pas la priorité*," which means drivers entering the roundabout do not have the right of way.

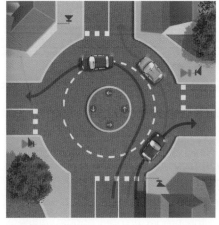

- When entering the roundabout, **do not** use your blinker.

- You cannot stop within the roundabout. If you miss your exit just go around and try again—but stay on the inside lane until you decide where you want to exit.

- When exiting the roundabout, **put on** your blinker.

GASOLINE – In France there are usually three types of fuel available:

- Super Sans Plomb (unleaded) 98 Octane

- Super Sans Plomb (unleaded) 95 Octane

- Diesel (Gazole)

Many gas stations are now self-service, so make sure you pick up the right pump. The diesel pump will always have a different color. Gassing up abroad is similar to how we do it at home: Just pick up the proper colored handle, place it in the tank, and start fueling. Pay in the office with cash or credit card.

Prices listed are per liter, a measurement of volume just over the size of a quart. So, it will take nearly 4 liters (3.79) to equal 1 gallon. If there is an attendant, the phrase "Fill 'er up" is *"Le plein, s'il vous plait."* (Forget all those words. Just say "Luh plan, sil voo play.")

When you've pumped the wrong fuel: If you've put in diesel instead of gas—or vice versa—**do not start** the vehicle. Tell the attendant immediately, as the tank will need to be drained. If you've already started to drive, your mistake will soon become painfully evident, as the engine will stop running. Walk back to the station and tell them the problem, if you haven't gone too far; otherwise call the car rental company.

NOTE: Gas will always be more expensive at the autoroute rest areas (aires). The cheapest place to buy gas is at the supermarkets (hypermarchés), which can be found all over France. Intermarché, Carrefour, Monoprix, Super U, and Géant Casino are a few of the most popular.

BREAKDOWNS AND ACCIDENTS

- On the autoroute: Orange SOS phones are located every 2 km / 1.2 mi. The operator will ask for the car location and description. If an accident has taken place, the operator will also ask whether the police or an ambulance is required.

- On other major roads: Orange SOS phones are located every 4 km / 2.5 mi.

EMERGENCY PHONE NUMBERS

- Police: 17

- Fire service (*Pompiers*) / Paramedics: 18 (like our 911)

- Ambulance (SAMU): 15

RADIO TRAFFIC CONDITIONS

A traffic update is broadcast hourly in English throughout the entire country on FM station 107.7.

PARKING

- Street Parking
  Do not park where curbs
  are painted yellow.

Parking

- Parking is free on the
  side of those roads with
  a broken white line or no
  markings at all.

- The Blue Zone (*Zone Bleu*) parking areas are
  operated in towns and cities. Time discs, which
  you display on the windshield, are available
  from tourist offices and tobacco (*tabac*) shops.

- Most large cities now
  have parking meters.
  Pay at the sidewalk
  ticket dispenser and
  place the ticket on the
  dash. Be sure your car is
  locked and the windows
  are rolled up tight.

Meter parking

- Attended and non-attended secure parking
  garages are located in major towns and cities.
  Tickets are dispensed from the ticket machines
  (*horodateurs*) upon entering, which you keep
  with you. On your return, payment is made at
  the payment machines, which require small
  bills or coin change and in turn spits out a vali-
  dated ticket that you insert in another machine
  at the exit.

BEST ADVICE: Trying to find street parking anywhere anytime is frustrating. Look for a secure parking garage so you don't have to worry about street or
time restrictions. If you're illegally parked you could
find a wheel clamp on your car when you return
that's guaranteed to ruin the rest of your day.

TRANSLATIONS

- Autres directions: Other directions
- Arrêt: Stop
- Bis: Alternative routing
- Bouchon: Traffic bottleneck
- Cédez le passage: Yield, give way
- Centre Ville: City or town center
- Écluse: Canal lock
- École: School
- Fermé: Closed
- Fin de chantier: End of road work
- Location de voiture: Car rental station
- Ouvert: Open
- Passage protégé: You have the right of way
- Passage piétons: Pedestrian crossing
- Péage: Toll
- Priorité à droite: Vehicles on the right have the right of way
- Rappel: Reminder—restriction still applies
- Sens interdit: No entry
- Sens unique: One way
- Secours: Emergency exit, help
- Sortie: Exit
- Suivres: Follow
- Toutes directions: All directions
- Transports d'Enfants: School bus
- Vous n'avez pas la priorité: You do not have the right of way
  - Droite: Right
  - Gauche: Left
  - Nord: North
  - Sud: South
  - Est: East
  - Ouest: West

POTPOURRI

TO AVOID THE AUTOROUTE

If you want to avoid the tolls and the speed of the autoroute, get yourself a **Bison Futé Map,** which are available free at most gas stations. These maps will show alternative recommended routes, usually noted as *"itineraire bis."*

BICYCLES

Biking is a national pastime—make that national mania—in France, and you'll find cyclists mainly in groups, mostly during weekends, on smaller roads in the hills and mountains. Their rights on the roads cannot be violated. If they sometimes tend to stray too far out on the road, it's probably because the edges are dangerous along that particular stretch. When you encounter cyclists, be considerate and patient—they have many more rights than you do!

TOUR DE FRANCE

Interested in following Le Tour? The complete route and detailed information pertaining to every facet of the race, is available each year in mid-May on the Tour Web site: **www.letour.fr**

TO PICNIC ENROUTE

If you're going to picnic in the French style—and you should—you need to plan ahead to buy your supplies.

Your most important stop will be the *boulange-rie*, the bakery selling breads, pastry, cakes, and sandwiches. Hours of operation typically run from 9 am to 12 noon or 1 pm, and again from around 4 pm to 6 pm. Closed Sundays. Plan on finding one before noon!

A *charcuterie* is a delicatessen-style butcher featuring various meats (mostly pork) sausage, confits, ham, and pates.

A *pâtisserie* sells the widest assortment of pastry that you'll ever encounter.

If you miss the time frame, look for an *épicerie* or *marché*, which are grocery stores.

Don't forget to have bottled water in the car at all times.

THE ESSENTIAL LIST FOR A PROPER FRENCH "PIQUE-NIQUE"

- Paper towels
- Paper plates
- Corkscrew
- Plastic wine glasses
- Bottled water/juice
- Paring knife (for fruit and bread)
- Mayonnaise and mustard in a tube
- Handy-wipes
- Tablecloth
- Tissue
- A package of small plastic zip baggies
- Small-size plastic garbage bags

You can purchase pique-nique utensil packs in most *marchés* (or buy one at home and bring it with you) consisting of small-size knives, forks, and spoons—usually four each— and a small, but adequate cutting board.

HANDY TRANSLATIONS TO HELP YOU KEEP OUT OF TROUBLE

Andouille or andouillette: This is a stew-like concoction containing various animal body parts including pork intestines, fat, sausage, pigs' tails, and chitterlings. Brutal!

Poulet, poularde, poule, poussin: These are ALL chicken, but don't confuse them with poulpe, which is octopus!!

Cuisses de grenouille: Frog legs

Langue: Tongue

Pieds de cochon: Pig's feet

Veau means veal, but téte de veau means calf's head!

Ris de veau or ris d'agneau: Sweetbreads

Cervelle de veau: Calf's brains

Rognon de veau: Kidneys

Tendrons de veau: Don't even ask

ITEMS YOU'LL WISH YOU'D BROUGHT WITH YOU

Small dashboard compass that attaches via a suction cup

Magnifying glass

Highlighter for maps, which make it much easier to keep track of your route

Small pair of binoculars (8 x 25 or 10 x 25)

Spare pens and pencils

Your own supply of ground coffee beans if you drink decaf coffee. Your hotel can use your supply to prepare your morning coffee. Decaf coffee in Europe is almost always Nescafé— definitely in the "yuk" category.

TAKING YOUR CAR TO ENGLAND?

The car-train service known as "Le Shuttle" carries vehicles and their occupants through the Channel Tunnel between Calais and Folkestone (near Dover.) The shuttle operates 24 hours a day, 7 days a week throughout the year. The trip takes 35 minutes at a top speed of 130 kph / 81 mph. From Paris, take the A 1 autoroute past Charles de Gaulle Airport to connect with the A 26 to Calais. As you approach Calais, you will begin to see signs that say "Le Shuttle" that will lead you to the terminal. After going through the tollbooth, you'll pass through customs to the departure area. You don't really need reservations, as departures are determined by volume, usually two to four per hour during the day and one per hour at night. If you want a confirmed reservation, call the information line at 0303 2711 00 or go online.

PUBLIC HOLIDAYS
Jan 1 – New Year's Day
Easter Sunday and Monday
Pentecost (7th Sunday after Easter)
Ascension Day (40 days after Easter)
May 1 – May Day
May 8 – VE Day (Victory in Europe – World War II)
July 14 – Bastille Day
August 15 – Assumption Day
November 1 – All Saints Day
November 11 – Armistice Day (World War I)
December 25 – Christmas Day

CURRENCY: The Euro

EMBASSIES
American Embassy
2 Avenue Gabriel, 75008 Paris
Tel. 01 43 12 22 22

American Consulate
Place Varian Fry, 13006 Marseilles
Tel 04 91 54 92 00

Canadian Embassy
35 Avenue Montaigne, 75008 Paris
Tel 01 44 43 29 00

CALLING THE USA OR CANADA:
Dial 001 + area code and number

CALLING THE UK:
Dial 0044 + area code and number

France

I T I N E R A R Y

DAY 1 PARIS TO HONFLEUR Via Giverny and Jumèiges

Michelin Regional Maps # 514 (Ile-de-France) and # 513 (Normandie)

IF YOU'RE COMING FROM CENTRAL PARIS

Starting in central Paris at the Place de la Concorde, drive straight up the Champs Élysées, keeping to the right-hand side of the avenue. As you approach the Arc de Triomphe (Étoile), move over to the far right lane. This leads you into the tunnel that takes you underneath the Arc and comes out on the other side, placing you onto the Avenue de la Grande Armée. Drive straight ahead into the large roundabout at the Porte (Pte.) Maillot. Circle around to the right and then bear around to the left and follow the white sign reading Périphérique Ouest then the white sign over the tunnel reading Périphérique Éxtérieur that leads into a "ring road" that completely encircles Paris. Once on the périphérique, stay in the middle or right lanes passing the exits for the Pte. Dauphine, the Pte. de la Muette, and the Pte. de Passy. Move into the far right lane and take the exit Pte. d'Auteuil, following the blue sign (general direction: ROUEN) leading to the A 13 autoroute (péage-toll).

Stay on the A 13 all the way to Exit # 14 toward the town of Bonnieres. However, at the bottom of the hill, follow the green sign for Vernon and drive along the river. When you see the bridge ahead of you, get into the left turn lane and turn left at the light, following the sign for Giverny. Drive up the hill to the bridge and turn right. Once on the other side, turn right again and follow the white sign for Giverny on D 5. After approximately 3 km / 2 mi the parking signs will start to appear. Those on the left will be closest to Monet's house and garden.

IF YOU'RE COMING FROM AIRPORT CHARLES DE GAULLE:

Leave the airport complex following the blue signs (general direction: PARIS). Then follow lane arrows for the A 86 to the A 14 that eventually becomes the A 13. Now go back to the previous paragraph and follow the directions given there.

It was at Giverny(☆) that Claude Monet decided to live and to satisfy his passions for painting, cultivating flowers, and photography. His garden is filled with thousands of flowers, carefully chosen for their matching colors, along with the famous Japanese bridge and the water lily-filled ponds.

Obviously the gardens are the main attraction here; however, the house provides an interesting look at country living during the turn of the last century. You will also see his collection of old Japanese prints, which he valued as inspirational, as well as reproductions of his own works. Expect long lines during the season.

Musée Claude Monet
(Monet's House and Garden)
Open daily except Mon., Apr. 1 to Oct. 31.
– 10 am to 6 pm.

Nearby is the American Impressionist Museum. Although not all that well known, this modern building houses a fine collection of American impressionist art with works by Winslow Homer, Mary Cassatt, Theodore Robinson, John Singer Sargent, and William Merritt Chase.

American Impressionist Museum
Open daily except Mon., Apr. 1 to Oct. 31.
– 10 am to 6 pm.

After your visit, go back the way you came in. At the roundabout (at the foot of the bridge you came in on), follow the sign (general direction: BEAUVAIS). After a couple of blocks, turn left at the light for Les Andelys on D 313. Keep following the white signs for Les Andelys until you reach the signs directing you to the parking area for the castle.

Dominated by the impressive ruins of the Château-Gaillard(☆☆), Les Andelys has one of the most commanding settings along the Seine. Richard the

Lionhearted, King of England and Duke of Normandy (Normandy was part of England in the 12th century), decided in 1196 to bar the King of France's way to Rouen along the Seine Valley by building this massive protective fortress on the cliff guarding and securing the river.

Château-Gaillard
Open mid Mar. to mid Nov. – Wed. 2 pm to 6 pm; Thu. through Mon. – 8:30 am to 12 noon and 2 pm to 6 pm. Closed Tue. and May 1.

After your visit, go out the way you came in and follow signs via Courcelles. Watch for the blue sign directing you to the A 13 autoroute (péage-toll) (general direction: ROUEN).

To avoid the autoroute, circle around Rouen to the south by using D 313 from Les Andelys via Courcelles to Gaillon, then take N 15 to Louviers where you follow signs (toutes directions or autres directions) to again pick up the D 313. Drive via Elbeuf and and Bourg-Achard. Next follow the sign (general direction: Caudebec-en-Caux) reading Route des Abbayes, all the way to the sign and right turn to Jumèiges leading to the little ferry that takes you across the Seine to the abbey.

If you took the autoroute, go all the way to Exit # 25. After the tollbooth, bear right and follow the sign for Caudebec-en-Caux and the Route des Abbayes on—you guessed it— D 313. After approximately 8 km / 5 mi, watch carefully for the signs for Jumèiges and the right turn leading down to the small ferry that takes you across the Seine. You most likely will have a short wait before making the ten-minute crossing.

Jumèiges(☆☆☆) The great abbey in its splendid setting on the Lower Seine forms one of the most powerful and commanding cluster of ruins in France. Founded in the 7th century by St. Philibert, within 50 years it housed a community of 700 monks and 1500 lay brothers. Destroyed by the Vikings in the 9th century, the abbey was rebuilt in the early 11th century by a new generation of builder abbots. The most striking feature of the abbey is the west façade with its two magnificent towers. Worth every one of its three stars.

Abbaye de Jumèiges
Open daily mid Apr. to mid Sep. – 9:30 am to 7 pm; mid Sep. to mid Apr. – 9:30 am to 1 pm and 2:30 pm to 5:30 pm. Closed Jan. 1, May 1, Nov. 11, and Dec. 25.

After your visit, go back toward the ferry but turn right on D 143 to connect with D 982 driving via the ancient (11th century) and pleasant riverside town of Caudebec-en-Caux(☆). From Caudebec, follow the signs to the Pont de Normandie (not to be confused with the Pont de Tancarville). Keep following the signs for the bridge. As you travel through an industrial area, don't worry if signs seem to disappear. Just continue straight until they start to appear again. Pay the bridge toll and cross over, following the sign for Honfleur. As you approach the town, follow signs for Centre Ville.

Honfleur(☆☆☆) (pop. 8,000), originally settled by the Vikings, was an important seaport town until the 15th century, and then acquired an important status in Europe when its mariners opened up trade routes through their 17th century Norman voyages of discovery. The character and atmosphere of Honfleur centers around the picturesque Vieux Bassin (old port) that has inspired painters, writers, and musicians for generations. Your first glance will tell you why.

JUST IN FOR THE DAY? The closest public parking is situated just as you enter the town. Follow the P parking sign to the right that leads you over a short bridge into a large parking area directly across from the town. If it's full, continue along the canal and take the next little bridge over into the town and turn right (the sign will read Trouville), which will take you to the other side of this small town where more parking can be found.

295 km / 183 mi

DAY 2 HONFLEUR TO BAYEUX

Michelin Regional Map # 513 (Normandie)

Leave Honfleur, drive west along the coast on D 513 via the fashionable seaside resort towns of Trouville and Deauville. Beginning in the mid- to late 1800s, the rich and famous beat the Paris heat by heading for the Côte Fleurie⭐⭐ (the Flower Coast) during the summer. Forced nowadays to share the wealthy clientele with the newer "in" places like Biarritz and the Riviera, this area has come down a peg or two from its fin-de-siecle sophistication but, nevertheless, is still packed in July and August.

This is probably enough sightseeing along the coast, so you want to be on your way to Bayeux. Continue along the sea via Villers-sur-Mer to Houlgate and follow the blue sign for the autoroute A 13 that will take you directly to the Caen Périphérique. Follow the sign for the Périphérique Nord, and take it around the city to Exit # 8, which will lead onto the N 13 straight to Bayeux.

NOTE: If you're not interested at all in the coast, just take the autoroute system from Honfleur (A 29) to the A 13 then to Exit # 8 and the N 13 to Bayeux. Fast and easy.

As you approach Bayeux, Exit # 36 will connect with the ring road that will have directions to where you need to be, i.e., Centre Ville, or one of the towns near the coast such as Port-en-Bessin, Sully, Crepon, Arromanches, etc.

POSSIBLE SLIGHT DETOUR: If you want to visit the The Caen Mémorial⭐⭐, as you approach the city follow the Mémorial signs.

This is the most comprehensive war museum ever assembled, with a complete overview of European history ranging from 1918 to the end of the "Cold

War." There is so much here to absorb that to do it properly would take an entire day.

However, if your main interest is the amazing story of the Normandy Beach invasions, it's best to save your time for the smaller D-Day Landing Museum located right on the beach in the seaside town of Arromanches near Omaha Beach. Visit this small museum tomorrow to lay the "groundwork" before exploring the beaches.

This afternoon try to visit the Bayeux Museum to see the famous Bayeux Tapestry(☆☆☆), as tomorrow will be spent along the invasion beaches and the American Cemetery at Omaha Beach.

Bayeux(☆☆) (pop. 15,000) was the first town liberated in France during the D-Day invasion—fortunately, and to everyone's relief, without destruction to its numerous Norman timbered houses, stone mansions, and cobbled streets. The great attraction here is the Bayeux Museum which contains the famous tapestry mentioned above depicting the Norman conquest of Britain in 1066. This mammoth piece of 11th century art, stitched with colored wools on a linen background, is 231 feet long by 19 inches high. It is the most precise and living document to come to us from the Middle Ages showing

The Normandy Invasion Beaches

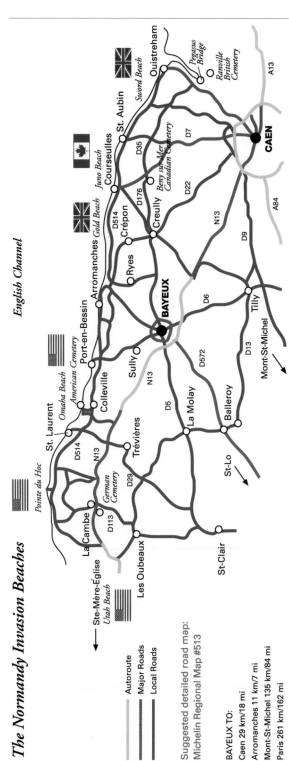

English Channel

Suggested detailed road map:
Michelin Regional Map #513

BAYEUX TO:
Caen 29 km/18 mi
Aromanches 11 km/7 mi
Mont-St-Michel 135 km/84 mi
Paris 261 km/162 mi

Autoroute
Major Roads
Local Roads

graphic details of the clothes, ships, arms, and customs of the period. Don't miss it!

Bayeux Museum
Open daily mid Mar. to early Nov. – 9 am to 6:30 pm (Open till 7 pm May to Aug.); early Nov. to mid Mar. – 9:30 am to 12:30 pm and 2 pm to 6 pm. Closed Jan. 1, 2, Dec. 25, and the morning of Dec. 26.

90 km / 56 mi

DAY 3 FULL DAY NORMANDY INVASION BEACHES☆☆☆

Michelin Regional Map # 513 (Normandie)

Get an early start today to have enough time to visit the many points of historical importance you must see here. Begin by driving down to Arromanches and following signs for the war museum, located on the beach, which will provide the all the essentials for an understanding of the momentous events that took place along these beaches on June 6, 1944.

Musée du Débarquement
Open daily May to Aug. – 9 am to 7 pm (Opens at 10 am Sun. in May.); Sep. – 9 am to 6 pm (Opens at 10 am on Sun.); Oct. to Apr. – 9:30 am to 12:30 pm and 1:30 pm to 5:30 pm. (Closes at 6 pm in Feb., Mar., and Apr.) Last admission 30 minutes before closing.

Closed Jan. and Christmas school holidays.

To stage a successful invasion along miles and miles of empty beaches, some sort of port facilities are needed to supply the invading troops with ammunition, trucks, and jeeps along with food, water, and medical supplies. In Normandy no suitable ports existed, so on the south coast of England, an extraordinary manufactured port was built of concrete sections. Immediately after the initial landings, these manmade dock sections were towed across the channel, linked together, and dropped in place just short of the beaches and...Voila! There's your port. The effort was dubbed Operation Mulberry, and even today, off the coast of Arromanches, you can still see remaining bits and chunks of this artificial military harbor sticking out of the water.

Omaha Beach was the most difficult and intensely fought-over beach on D-Day because the heavily fortified cliffs overlooking the beach were controlled by the Germans. On the morning of June 6, 1944, American landing craft headed for these cliffs, but because of heavy enemy fire and rough seas, only a few were able to successfully reach the shore. The initial landings are remembered mainly for the 2,400 casualties American soldiers suffered on this beach. Nevertheless, an important "foothold" had been established, and by the end of the day 34,000 troops had been landed. For Hitler, the handwriting was clearly "on the wall." The American Military Cemetery contains 9,000 perfectly aligned white crosses made of Carrera marble. A chapel and a memorial dedicated to the fallen young men complete what no doubt will be a highly emotional experience for you.

Go back to D 14, turn right, and follow the signs for the **Pointe du Hoc**. The most dramatic assault of the D-Day Invasion took place here where 225 rangers scaled the 130-foot-high cliff with the help of grappling hooks—a technique right out of the Middle Ages—in an attempt to knock out the German heavy gun emplacements that were bombarding the main land section of the beach some 7 miles away. They suffered 75% casualties during the 48-hour battle, but finally prevailed. The land on this site lies undisturbed from June 6, 1944, and the bomb craters can be seen everywhere on the site along with the German machine gun and long-range canon concrete bunkers. A rough-hewn stone monument, standing like a megalith overlooking the sea, honors Colonel Rudder's heroic Ranger Commandos.

DAY 4 BAYEUX TO MONT-ST-MICHEL

Michelin Regional Map # 513 (Normandie)

NOTE: The ring road around Bayeux is, in some parts, not very well defined, and so it tends to lack the adequate directional signs. With that in mind, wherever you're leaving from in the vicinity, get your hotel to help you hook up with the D 6 south via Tilly and Villers-Bocage. leading to the A 84 autoroute (general direction: RENNES).

A 84 will end just north at Avranches. After the toll, keep driving south (general direction: FOUGÈRES and RENNES) now on N 175. As you approach Exit # 34, follow the signs for Le Mont-St-Michel.

If you prefer a non-toll route, drive from Bayeux via St-Lo, Coustance, and Granville to Mont-St-Michel.

All parking is out at the end of the causeway. Signs at the parking entrance will advise high tide details and any possible risks involved. If you're staying overnight at one of the few hotels located on the Mont, the hotel will send porters down to your car for the luggage. There are also hotels nearby located 2 km south at La Digue. The Relais St-Michel is a nice four-star hotel with dramatic views looking back at the Mont.

This is an extraordinary place, but it's unique as an overnight stop. Because of its physical makeup, the Mont has only a few hotels, including the famous La Mere Poulard whose restaurant is known the world over for its fabulous omelettes, savored by rich and poor alike since 1888.

Le Mont-St-Michel(☆☆☆) is possibly the most important historic monument in Europe, and one of the great architectural sites of the world. The Mont is composed of a small island with an extraordinary superstructure that has been raised over the centuries. It has remained intact over time and contains buildings of all ages and styles. Most noteworthy among these is the great monastery known as La Merveille (The Marvel).

BEST ADVICE: Almost all year long this is a very crowded place with a decidedly cheap commercial aspect in its lower reaches around the entrance during the day. However, at night, it becomes a very serene and quiet place that presents an entirely different perspective and atmosphere. If you decide not to overnight in this area, continue on to nearby St-Malo or Dinard, where a full range of accommodations are available.

135 km / 84 mi

DAY 5 MONT-ST-MICHEL TO THE CHÂTEAUX COUNTRY (Saumur)

Michelin Regional Maps # 513 (Normandie) and # 517 (Pays de la Loire)

This is a day to get quickly down to the banks of the Loire River between the towns of Angers and Saumur. From Mont-St-Michel, take D 976 / N 175 via Pontorson south towards Rennes. Coming into Rennes, follow the signs leading you around the city for Laval on N 157. As you approach the city, look for signs to take you south via Château-Gontier to Angers on N 162.

As you cross the river, you'll see the castle off on your left. Enter Angers, get in the right lane, and follow the white sign for château parking. At the stoplight turn right onto the Boulevard Général de Gaulle. Passing the castle again (still on your left), get in the right lane and proceed to the next light, where you turn right into the parking lot. These lots are not all that big, so if they're full, just get back on Bd. de Gaulle and about a block or two further on, you will see an electronic parking sign on the left-hand side of the street directing you to a larger parking facility. The sign will also indicate whether the lot is available (green light) or full (red light).

Built on a Roman foundation, Angers(☆☆☆) remains one of the great examples of a no-nonsense medieval fortress castle. With 17 towers and a system of moats, along with its strategic position overlooking the river, Angers presents a formidable bastion that protected its inhabitants for more than 800 years.

Also of great importance here is the extraordinary Apocalypse(☆☆☆) tapestry that was commissioned in 1373 by the Duke of Anjou and illustrates the last book of the Bible. Exceptional for its stylistic and technical qualities, this amazing giant piece of medieval art is as long as a football field, stands 15 feet tall, and depicts 70 scenes. It is the oldest tapestry of this size in existence anywhere in the world.

Château d'Angers
Open daily Jun. to mid Sep. – 9:30 am to 7 pm; mid Sep. to end Oct. and mid Mar. to end May – 10 am to 6 pm; Nov. to mid Mar. – 10 am to 5 pm. Last admission 45 minutes before closing. Closed Jan. 1, May 1, Nov. 11, and Dec. 25.

Guided tours available from the tourist office located at the Place du Kennedy near the entrance to the château.

After your visit, get back on the Bd. de Gaulle driving south, which is away from the river. The boulevard will change names from de Gaulle to rue Paul Bert and eventually to rue Volney. Keep straight following the signs for Trélazé and Saumur then white signs reading Saumur Touristique, taking you along the north bank of the Loire on D 952. Stay on D 952 to the village of les Rosiers, where you turn right, travel over the bridge to Gennes, then turn left, so you are now driving on the south bank of the Loire on D 751.

The Loire Valley(☆☆☆), also known as La Vallée des Rois—the Valley of the Kings— presents possibly the most fascinating and historic landscape in Europe. Here you will find castles and grand manor houses covering the entire medieval era and encompassing every conceivable style of architecture, from massive fortresses complete with moats and drawbridges built for war and siege to lacy-turreted fairytale castles. And an amazing cast of famous characters have left their mark in this valley, including Julius Caesar, Attila the Hun, Richard the Lionhearted, and Joan of Arc. Nowhere else in the world can such a marvelous range of castles, fortresses, palaces, monastic buildings, and abbeys be visited within such a relatively small area.

The most important buildings and castles in the valley all date from different periods. Those of Angers, Chinon, and Langeais were built in medieval times. Those dating from the Renaissance include Amboise, Azay-le-Rideau, Blois, Chambord, Chaumont, Chenonceau, Ussé, and Villandry. Those built later in the 17th and 18th century in neoclassical style include Cheverny and Valençay.

BEST ADVICE: During your time in the Loire Valley, avoid the sprawling commercial city of Tours and stay in one of the small towns or villages outside along the river.

290 km / 180 mi

DAY 6 EXPLORING THE CHÂTEAUX COUNTRY (Saumur to Amboise)

Michelin Regional Map # 517 (Pays de la Loire)

Grammar note: Château = singular – Châteaux = plural

Even though the distances between the châteaux are not great, adequate time must be allowed to fully enjoy your visit. The problem (if you can call it that) is which ones you should visit both from the outside as well as the inside, and how many you can visit comfortably in one day. The answer

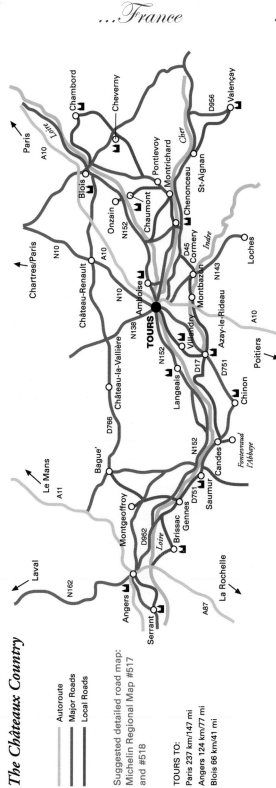

The Châteaux Country

Autoroute
Major Roads
Local Roads

Suggested detailed road map:
Michelin Regional Map #517
and #518

TOURS TO:
Paris 237 km/147 mi
Angers 124 km/77 mi
Blois 66 km/41 mi

MONT-ST-MICHEL TO THE CHÂTEAUX COUNTRY

to that, of course, depends on you, and your level of interest and energy, but we have found it possible to visit three or four in any single day. For those who prefer a more relaxed schedule, one in the morning and one in the afternoon works well. There are lots of combinations to consider depending on your time and schedule. There will be some unavoidable back-tracking, but distances are short, so don't let this be a concern.

BEST ADVICE: For those who want in-depth information, the best publication is the Michelin Green Guide, *Châteaux of the Loire.*

Here's an example for the relatively short drive from the eastern sector to the western.

Drive east along the south bank of the Loire on D 947 toward Montsoreau, then follow the signs to Fontevraud l'Abbaye(☆☆). Signs will lead you to the parking areas.

Founded in 1101, this was one of the largest monastic complexes in the Western World.

First make a visit inside to the abbey to see the final resting places of the most powerful and intriguing couple of the Middle Ages: King Henry II of England and Eleanor of Aquitaine, as well as their eldest son, Richard the Lionhearted. One of their other sons, wicked King John of Magna Carta fame, was the pursuer of that rascal, Robin Hood, immortalized in film by the dashing actor, Errol Flynn. Together Henry and Eleanor's domains extended from the Scottish border to the Pyrenees. A wonderful movie, *The Lion in Winter*, depicted the latter stages of their lives and starred Katharine Hepburn and Peter O'Toole—talk about perfect casting! The other point of interest here is the abbey that contains the only remaining example of a true Romanesque kitchen(☆☆). Built around 1160, this medieval kitchen has cooking paraphernalia and multiple chimney features not seen elsewhere. A short but altogether unique visit.

Fontevraud l'Abbaye
Open daily Jun. to Sep. – 9 am to 6:30 pm.; Oct., Apr., and May – 10 am to 6 pm; Nov. to Mar. – 10 am to 5:30 pm. Closed Jan. 1, Nov. 11, and Dec. 25.

From Fontevraud, drive toward the river and onto D 751, following signs for Candes to pick up the D 7 eastbound along the river. After traveling 8 km from Candes, turn left across the river (general direction: BOURGUEIL). Once over the bridge, turn right on N 152 to Langeais, following the brown château signs to the free parking.

Built in 1491, the Château de Langeais(☆☆) is one of the finest feudal military buildings remaining from the late Middle Ages. For a close-up history lesson, this château requires an inside visit. All of the apartments(☆☆☆) in the castle are furnished in their original style, including a unique collection of 15th century tapestries. A kind of wax museum in the Great Hall depicts the historically important marriage of Charles VIII and Anne of Brittany. In the nearby park of the château stand the ruins of a strategic "keep," built in 994 and considered to be the oldest structure of its kind in the entire country.

Château de Langeais
Open daily Apr. to Sep. – 9 am to 6:30 pm. (Open till 9 pm mid Jul. to end Aug.); Oct. – 9 am to 12:30 pm and 2 pm to 6:30 pm; Nov. to Mar. – 9 am to 12 noon and 2 pm to 5 pm. Closed Dec. 6 and 25.

MONT-ST-MICHEL TO THE CHÂTEAUX COUNTRY

After your visit, follow signs that will take you back across the river on D 57 to the elegant Azay-le-Rideau(★★★). This stunning château was built between 1518 and 1527, and by all accounts, is the most graceful example of early Renaissance architecture that exists in France. Rising in part from the very riverbed of the Indre, the château features dramatic white walls and gray-blue slates that are mirrored in the calm waters of this gentle waterway. An inside visit is fairly interesting, but not essential—it's the exterior that's important here. Don't forget your camera.

Free parking is found in a variety of lots in the village around the château.

Azay-le-Rideau
Open daily Apr. to Oct. – 9:30 am to 6 pm. (Open till 7 pm Jul. and Aug.) Closed Jan. 1, May 1, Nov. 11, and Dec. 25.

NOTE: Remember, the latest visitors are admitted in most châteaux is usually 45 minutes before closing.

From Azay-le-Rideau, drive east out of the village following the signs to Artannes on D 84, then Montbazon on D 17. As you come into the middle of the town, D 17 will intersect with the major highway N 10 at the stoplight. Turn left, then stay to the right for a block or two. At the light, turn right and follow the sign reading Veigné; you are now back on D 17. Stay on this road for 10 km / 6 mi until you intersect with N 143. Turn right, direction Comery, but after just a kilometer or so, watch for the left turn for Bleré on D 45. After 13 km / 8 mi you will intersect with N 76. Turn right following the sign to Bleré. After 2.5 km, follow the signs for Amboise on D 31, which will lead you to the Centre.

BEST ADVICE: If you're looking for a "home base" from which to explore this sector of the Châteaux Country, Amboise would be your best choice because of its central location and abundance of accommodations.

130 km / 81 mi

DAY 7 THE CHÂTEAUX COUNTRY (Amboise, Blois, Chenonceau)

Michelin Regional Map # 518 (Centre)

The mighty fortress château of Amboise☆☆ (pop. 11,500) is amassed on the rock above the river, with the houses of the town clustered about at its feet. Of all the dark memories associated with this château, the public execution by the Catholics of 1,200 Protestant Huguenots during the French Wars of Religion in 1560 is the historical event for which it's most remembered. However, the greatest interest here is the different architectural styles of the château, the park-like grounds, and the expansive river views surrounding the fortress—and a little-known association with Leonardo da Vinci.

> **Château d'Amboise**
> Open daily mid Mar. to end Mar. – 9 am to 6 pm; Apr. to Jun. – 9 am to 6:30 pm (Jul. and Aug. open till 7 pm.); Sep. and Oct. – 9 am to 6 pm; Nov. to end Jan. – 9 am to 12 noon and 2 pm to 4:45 pm; Feb. to mid Mar. – 9 am to 12 noon and 1:30 pm to 5:30 pm (Closes at 4:45 pm in Jan.) Times subject to change. Closed Jan. 1 and Dec. 25.

A Last Look at Leonardo

For a very personal glimpse into one of history's greatest minds, drive just a few kilometers up the road from Amboise via rue Victor Hugo to the Clos-Lucé (clo-loo-say), the last home of Leonardo da Vinci. Invited to Amboise by François I, France's king in 1516, Da Vinci lived and worked at Clos-Lucé until his death in 1519. The basement of the house contains scale models of some 40 of his inventions, including an airplane, a parachute (can't be too careful), tanks, and a forerunner to the WW II machine gun. Michelin gives it only one star, but it's definitely worth an inside visit. After all, it IS Leonardo! And you'll even see the bed in which he died.

Le Clos-Lucé

Le Clos-Lucé
Open daily Feb. through Dec. – 9 am to 7 pm (Open till 8 pm Jul. and Aug.); Jan. – 10 am to 5 pm. Closed Jan. 1 and Dec. 25.

After your visit, cross the bridge in the middle of town and turn right on N 152 for Blois.

As you approach the city on N 152, watch for the left turn signs for the underground parking garage just below the castle. This will be the most convenient parking you will find.

BEST ADVICE: If this garage shows a red-lit sign, the lot is full. Keep going straight for more parking spots on your right along the river, although these are limited in number.

Historically, Blois(☆☆) (pop. 50,000) is as important as just about any château in the valley and definitely worth an inside visit. Names from its past include Joan of Arc, whose banner was consecrated here before engaging the English invaders in battle. Cardinal Richelieu plotted political intrigue here, and the conspiratorial Caesar Borgia once roamed its halls representing the "interests" of the pope. The most famous event here, however, was the murder of the Duke de Guise during The Wars of Religion. Best to get all the gory details and their implications inside the château itself.

Château de Blois
Open daily Apr. to Sep. – 9 am to 6 pm; Sep. to Mar. – 9:30 am to 12:30 pm and 2 pm to 5 pm. Closed Jan 1. and Dec. 25.

MONT-ST-MICHEL TO THE CHÂTEAUX COUNTRY

The city of Blois is a very interesting place in its own right with pedestrian-only walking streets, a wonderful old town with houses and public buildings from the Middle Ages and a host of atmospheric restaurants.

After your visit, cross the bridge nearest the castle, Pont J. Gabrial, and follow the sign for Pontlevoy and Montrichard on N 751 / D764. From Montrichard, follow directions to D 176 along the river to the village of Chenonceaux and then signs to the château.

A huge free parking lot is located on the grounds in front of the château.

NOTE: The village of Chenonceaux is spelled with an "x" and the Château de Chenonceau without.

The truly unique Château de Chenonceau(☆☆☆), a jewel in the crown of Renaissance architecture, was built gracefully over the River Cher in 1513 and is known as the château of "Six Women" for the leading roles its hostesses have played for over 400 years. After crossing a drawbridge, you reach a terrace surrounded by moats. To the left is Diane de Poitiers' Italian garden; to the right, the garden of Catherine dé Medici is bounded by the massive trees of the park. An interesting wax museum located on the grounds re-creates the story of Chenonceau and the influence of its remarkable ladies who include Louise de Lorraine and, of all people, Mary Queen of Scots. Inside and outside visits are highly recommended. Be sure you allow time for both.

BEST ADVICE. Since this is one of the most visited sites in France, try to be there early in the day or in the late afternoon to avoid at least some of the tour buses. Today's suggested itinerary is routed to make Chenonceau the last stop.

Château de Chenonceau
Open daily Mar. 1 to mid Sep. – 9 am to 7 pm. (Closes at 6 pm first two weeks in Mar.); mid Sep. to end Oct. – 9 am to 6 pm. (Closes at 5:30 pm first two weeks in Oct.); Nov. 1 to end Jan.– 9 am to 4:30 pm; Feb. – 9 am to 5 pm. Times subject to change.

After your visit follow signs out of the parking lot area back to your base. If you're staying around

Amboise, take either the back road D 81 right out of Chenonceaux or the main road D 31, which you can pick up a little further east along the river.

DAY 8 THE CHÂTEAUX COUNTRY (Chaumont, Chambord, and Cheverny)

Michelin Regional Map #518 (Centre)

Leave Amboise this morning driving along the south bank of the Loire on D 751 via Mosnes to Chaumont. Follow the sign leading to the château entrance, but continue straight ahead to the river where you will find free parking.

Rising sheer from the banks of the Loire, the Château de Chaumont(☆☆) dominates the village below. The castle is very fortress-like, with its four wide towers, a sentry walk, and a drawbridge. In 1560 Catherine dé Medici, widow of King Henri II, acquired the castle and installed her Italian astrologer in a room connected by a secret stairway to the top of a tower used as an observatory where together they consulted the stars. Later, in an act of revenge, the queen exchanged feudal Chaumont for graceful Chenonceau, residence of Diane de Poitiers, mistress of the late king. The apartments of both women contain medieval tapestries and fine period furniture. The fascinating gardens surrounding the castle are reworked every year and a new theme is adopted to create a botanical landscape of imagination and originally. Unique!

Château de Chaumont

Open daily Apr. to early May and mid to late Sep. – 10:30 am to 5:30 pm; early May to mid Sep. – 9:30 am to 6:30 pm; Oct. to Mar. – 10 am to 5 pm. Times subject to change.

MONT-ST-MICHEL TO THE CHÂTEAUX COUNTRY

NOTE: If you're interested in an exterior look only, the park is open daily all year from 9 am till dusk. No admission charge.

Château and park closed Jan. 1, May 1, Nov. 11, and Dec. 25.

After your visit, drive east on D 751 via Cande staying on the south side of the river, driving towards Blois. Signs will soon appear for Chambord. The road patterns around here are very tricky, but just keep heading east and you'll be fine.

Château de Chambord(☆☆☆) was the favorite hunting retreat of François I built in 1556 on the edge of the Forest of Boulogne, just eight kilometers from the Loire River. With some 440 rooms, this is the largest and most flamboyant of all of the châteaux in the region. Architecturally (it is said that Leonardo da Vinci had a hand in the original design), it appears as a fortress with an enormous central keep flanked by huge wings and corner towers. If you go inside this showplace you'll find an extraordinary double-spiral stair-case which is so constructed that two people can pass up and down without seeing each other. All in all, I can't think of anything quite like it anywhere else in Europe.

Château de Chambord
Open daily Apr. to Sep. – 9 am to 6:30 pm; Jul. and Aug. – 9:30 am to 6:45 pm; Oct. to Mar. – 9 am to 5:30 pm; Closed Jan. 1, May 1, and Dec. 25. Last admission 30 minutes before closing. Times subject to change.

After your visit, depart from the park southbound following signs for Bracieux on D 112. Drive through the town and watch for the right turn to Cour-Cheverny. Continue through the village following the brown signs leading to the château. Areas for parking are indicated on the pavement.

Château de Cheverny(☆☆☆) is different in style and use than anything you've seen thus far. It was built in 1634, rather late as most châteaux go, in classical style as a residence for the family of the local count. Here, almost more than any other château, an inside visit is important. The splendor of the interior decoration and furniture makes it a miniature Versailles. The overall beauty, both inside and out, is made complete by the surrounding park with its gardens, tall trees and water features.

Château de Cheverny
Open daily Apr. to Sep. – 9:15 am to 6:15 pm (Open till 6:45 pm Jul. and Aug.); Oct. to Mar. – 9:15 am to12 noon and 2:15 pm to 5 pm. (Open till 5:30 pm Mar. and Oct.)

If you're a dog fancier, then you'll probably be interested in the "**feeding of the hounds**," which takes place every afternoon during the season. The hunting tradition is alive and well here at Cheverny, and the feeding ritual of these 90 highly trained crossbred hunters is a sight to behold. You can see the dogs anytime the château is open, but "dinner time" is a hoot. Be sure to have your camera—just remember some of your pictures may end up being X-rated.

Feeding of the Hounds
Apr. to mid Sep. daily at 5 p.m.; Mid Sep. to end Mar. – daily at 3 p.m. except Tue., Sat., Sun., and public holidays.

If you want to take the quickest route back to the Amboise area, follow signs for the D 52 driving via Sambin and Pontlevoy to Montrichard. From here, follow signs for Amboise via D 115 / D 61.

SOUND AND LIGHT SHOWS

A few of the Loire's historic châteaux are enhanced during the summer months by evening spectacles known as Son et Lumière (Sound and Light). The building's history is illustrated by a sequence of color floodlighting accompanied by music, actors in period costume, and special effects. Four of the most popular are as follows:

AMBOISE
The show, "At the Court of François I," features a cast of 400 locals with lots of high-tech lighting features plus music and fireworks makes for a very lavish production.

Open Wed. and Sat. from late Jun. to the end of Aug., with performances starting at 10:30 pm (10 pm in Aug.) lasting 1 hour 45 minutes.

AZAY-LE-RIDEAU
In a leisurely "walk around" format, this show creates a mystical atmosphere by illuminating turrets and towers of this fairytale

castle, accompanied by music drifting out of the surrounding park.

Open nightly at 10:30 pm from the first of May till the end of Sep. Gates open at 10:30 pm in May, Jun., and Jul., 10 pm in Aug., and 9:30 pm in Sep.

BLOIS

This château gives a thousand-year history lesson complete with visual effects, special lighting, and a unique sound system make for a spirited and entertaining evening.

Open every evening from the end of Apr. to the middle of Sep., starting between 9:30 pm and 10:30 pm. Lasts 45 minutes.

CHENONCEAU

In "The Ladies of Chenonceau" (Au temps des Dames de Chenonceau), the evolution of this "most beautiful château" by Catherine Briçonnet, Diane de Poitiers, and Catherine dé Medici is portrayed.

Open nightly from Jul. 1 to Aug. 31 at 10:15 pm.

Other châteaux offering sound and light shows include Loches and Valençay.

BEST ADVICE: Check with the local tourist office (or your hotel) to confirm times.

DAY 9 CHÂTEAUX COUNTRY TO THE DORDOGNE

Michelin Regional Maps # 518 (Centre) and # 524 (Aquitaine)

An early start is required today to get down to the Dordogne, and the best way to speed up this process is by using the A 10 autoroute (péage-toll) from Tours to Poitiers and then the N 10 down to Angoulême followed by the "back roads" into the Dordogne.

From the Amboise area, stay on this side of the river, taking D 751 to Tours. Follow the blue péage sign for the A 10 autoroute (general direction: POITIERS).

A reminder for those who want to avoid the toll autoroutes: You can pick up the N 10 that runs parallel to the A 10, using this same route into Tours, but following the green signs for Poitiers.

Once past Poitiers, the A 10 becomes the N 10 and the autoroute goes off our screen. Continue south on N 10 to Angoulême. Since there is no way to avoid the city itself, just follow the signs Toutes Directions and then signs for Brantôme and Périgueux on D 939. Once in Périgueux, look for Autre Directions (general direction: BRIVE). Coming out of Périgueux, you will be on the N 221. After six or seven kilometers, signs will lead you briefly onto the N 89, directing you to the D 710 (general direction: SARLAT). Stay on the D 710 for about 15 km / 9 mi and take the left fork in the road to the D 47 direct to Les Eyzies(☆☆). (pop. 950)

The capital of prehistory lies at the base of a unique setting of steep cliffs located at the confluence of two rivers, the Vézere and the Beune. It was here in 1868 that workers leveling the soil for a railroad track unearthed the Cro-Magnon cave skeletons. Main sites here are the Museum of Prehistory (☆)

and the Grand-Roc Grotto (✩✩✩). Because of its prehistoric importance, this town will be packed with tourists during the summer months, and most especially in July and August. Guided tours of the caves are by appointment only (no matter what time of year), and the number of visitors allowed each day is limited. Caves and museums are always closed on Tuesday. If you are really interested in visiting one or two of the caves, you definitely need to preplan your visit.

Cro-Magnon man and descendant

The ancient market town of Sarlat(✩✩✩) (pop. 11,000) is right out of the Middle Ages, and is the largest and most important in the Perigord region. Lots of old buildings and houses loaded with character rate it three Michelin stars. Sarlat is a good choice to use as a base for those who wish to spend more time exploring the Dordogne. Parking can be found only on the perimeter of the town, near the church. Follow the blue parking signs.

350 km / 217 mi

DAY 10 THE DORDOGNE TO ROCAMADOUR

Michelin Regional Map # 524 (Aquitaine)

From the Les Eyzies area, follow the signs for St-Cyprien, then the sign for the riverside village of Beynac(☆). The Counts of Beynac erected a formidable fortress château(☆☆) in one of the most splendid situations of the entire Dordogne Valley. If you want to see a close-up of castle life in the 13th century, this one is hard to beat. Follow signs up the hill to the castle.

If you're in need of some exercise and are a good walker, the castle can also be reached by a steep footpath called the Caminal del Panieraire(☆), which meanders up through the medieval village(☆) to reach the castle and church overlooking a vast panorama(☆☆) of the river valley.

THE DORDOGNE VALLEY(★★★)

The diversity and sheer beauty of the landscape through which this river flows, and the architectural glories that overlook its banks, make this remarkable valley one of the most agreeable areas of exploration in the country.

Two gentlemen from the Dordogne

From Beynac, stay on the D 703 to the village of La Roque-Gageac(★★), nestled under a sheer rock cliff that drops right down to the river. Stay on the D 703 via Carsac to Souillac. As you drive through the town, follow the green signs for the N 20 to Payrac (general direction: CAHORS/GOURDON). After approximately 16 km / 10 mi, you will reach the town of Payrac where you follow the signs and make a left turn for Rocamadour along the twisting D 673.

Built right into a steep rock-face in the gorge of the Aizon River, the gravity-defying village of Rocamadour(★★★) (pop. 650) is dominated by its 14th century castle and ecclesiastical center dating from the late 12th century. In some ways it's rather like Mont-St-Michel—much better in the evening after the day-trippers have left. There are a few hotels in the town, but most are nearby at the edge of the village.

DORDOGNE TO ROCAMADOUR

IF YOU'RE JUST IN FOR THE DAY: The single street through the town is pedestrian-only, so parking is either at the base of the cliff or at the top of the cliff behind the site.

Lifts and stairs get you to where you need to be. This is one of France's most unusual places of pilgrimage.

BEST ADVICE: Because Rocamadour is overrun by tourists during the high season, try to visit either in early spring or late fall. Otherwise, the earlier in the day the better.

110 km / 71 mi

DAY 11 ROCAMADOUR TO THE TARN GORGE

Michelin Regional Map # 525 (Midi-Pyrénées)

Leave Rocamadour this morning driving east to pick up the N 140 where you turn right and follow the signs (general direction: RODEZ) via Figeac and Decazeville.

SIDE TRIP TO CONQUES. About 8 km / 5 mi past Decazeville, watch for the left turnoff to Conques(☆☆) (pop. 300). This tiny medieval village boasts a beautiful hilly setting and one of the oldest Romanesque churches (☆☆) on the ancient pilgrimage route to Santiago de Compostella in

Spain. The tympanum above the west door deserves accolades (⭐⭐⭐) for its stone reproduction of the Last Judgment that dates back to 1135 and demonstrates this site's architectural importance. And inside the church, the Tresor (treasury)(⭐⭐⭐) contains some of the most important religious art objects in Europe dating back to the 7th century. If you have any interest at all in medieval art, this remote little place is definitely worth a detour.

The Trésor
Open daily – 9 am to 12 noon and 2 pm to 6 pm (Open till 7 pm Jul. and Aug.) Closed Jan. 1.

NOTE: You might consider bypassing the overnight in Rocamadour and staying in this tiny, but historically important village. There are two nice small places here: Hotel Ste-Foy, and the Auberge St-Jacques, plus Le Moulin de Cambelong located three kilometers south of the village on D 901. Booking early is essential.

Drive back to the N 140, turn left, and follow the signs for Rodez. From Rodez follow the signs for Millau, driving via Laissac on N 88. Approximately 20 km / 12 mi from Laissace, you approach Sévérac-le-Château where the signs reading Gorges du Tarn start to appear. Follow signs for Le Massegros (passing underneath the north/south-running A 75 autoroute) and the Gorges du Tarn on D 995.

NOTE: The last seven or eight kilometers into the gorge will be very steep with a number of hairpin turns. The road number through the gorge is D 907 Bis.

The Tarn Gorge(⭐⭐⭐) is undoubtedly one of the most striking features in France. The valley was carved out in a number of different phases, the last one extending over a million years. Sheer cliffs tower above the valley bottom to heights of up to 500 meters, offering a constantly changing succession of views of dramatic proportion. What makes the Tarn different from other natural sites, other than the fact that the road was blasted out of the overhanging cliffs, is that an active life goes on within the gorge itself. At one time in the distant past, people lived and somehow eked out an existence deep in the gorge along the river. Today, water sports and other activities are plentiful.

Rocamadour to mid Tarn Gorge (La Malène)
185 km / 115 mi

Side trip to Conques add 30 km /19 mi

BEST ADVICE: Check out two exceptional hotels in the gorge both near La Malène. The Chateau de la Caze a majestic castle dating from the 15th century, and is in a class by itself, but with only twenty rooms. Expensive. The Manoir de Montesquiou is an ancient manor house also dating from the 15th century with twelve rooms. Moderate.

Other places to stay in the gorge include the small towns of La Malène (pop. 175) and Ste-Enimie (pop. 500). Hotels are few and far between. Unless you have reserved a place to stay, it's possible every place will be full when you get there. In that case, you'll have to continue through the gorge to either Florac or Alès—both of which have only a few hotels. Failing that (deep sigh), you'll need to head for Nîmes.

La Malène to Florac (past the end of the gorge)
41 km / 25 mi

Florac to Alès 70 km / 43 mi

Alès to Pont du Gard 51 km / 32 mi

DAY 12 TARN GORGE TO PROVENCE (via the Pont du Gard)

Michelin Regional Map # 526 (Languedoc-Roussillon)

The N 106 will take you from Florac to Alès. Continue through Alès following signs for Avignon, Nîmes, and Uzès. Eventually signs will read Uzès / Avignon via D 981.

Uzès(☆☆)(pop. 8.000) is a well-preserved medieval fortress town straight out of the Middle Ages. Classified as a "Ville d'art et d'histoire," this 16th century stronghold has faithfully restored its vielle ville (old town) to the era when its prosperity was made possible by the manufacture of silk and linen. Not a well-known destination, but a jewel nonetheless.

For a visit, the one-way ring road will lead you to the parking areas that will be just a short walk to the old section of the town.

From Uzès, follow signs for Avignon on the D 981 that will lead you to the Pont du Gard.

Follow the blue P sign for parking on the left bank (rive gauche) of the river. Between the aqueduct bridge and the parking lot is La Grande Expo, which features a fascinating exhibition describing every aspect relating to this magnificent structure.

The Pont du Gard(☆☆☆) is truly one of the great wonders of the Roman world. This magnificent three-tiered aqueduct was built in 19 B.C. to form a part of a water-carrying system of some 30 miles, stretching from springs near Uzès to the then expanding Roman city of Nîmes. It's almost 1,000 feet long and 160 feet high. The huge blocks of stone weigh up to six tons each and were put into place without the use of mortar. This commanding structure is the finest surviving example of Roman architecture that exists in Europe.

When you leave the parking lot, signs will direct you to:

Nîmes: 25 km / 16 mi via the N 86

Arles: 40 km / 25 mi via Beaucaire and Tarascon

Avignon: 26 km / 16 mi via N 100

NÎMES(☆☆☆) (pop. 135,000)

In its early history, this was a Roman colony of handsome temples, an Amphitheatre (arènas) (☆☆☆), a basilica, a forum, several baths, and a long line of fortifications. The most graceful of the Roman remains is the Maison Carrée (☆☆☆), an exquisite temple beautifully preserved that was dedicated to the adopted sons of Emperor Augustus.

IF YOU'RE JUST IN NÎMES FOR THE DAY: Two large parking garages can be found across from the Maison Carrée on the rue General Perrier. There is also a large underground parking just to the east side of the Roman Arena.

ARLES(✩✩✩) (pop. 52,000)

This Gallo-Roman city is located on one of the four major pilgrimage routes to Santiago de Compostella in Spain. Arles is smaller and more manageable than either Nîmes or Avignon. The highlights here are the Roman theatre(✩✩), the Amphitheatre(✩✩), and the cathedral of St-Trophime(✩), which was founded in the 4th century and includes a Romanesque nave and a 12th century portal(✩✩) renowned as a masterpiece of Provençal sculpture. Arles has a cozy and intimate feel—a great place to use as a home base.

IF YOU'RE JUST IN ARLES FOR THE DAY: Two large parking garages can be found on the south side of the city along the Bd. Clemenceau / Bd. des Lices near the tourist office.

AVIGNON(✩✩✩) (pop. 250,000)

Avignon's early claim to fame came during 1309 to 1377, when it was the residence of the popes and reached the height of its importance among the cities of Provence. Seven popes reigned here until the revolution of 1791, when Avignon was formally declared once more united to France. The most important site here is the Palais des Papes(✩✩✩). Originally a prosperous Roman colony, Avignon has been surrounded by its magnificent fortified walls since the Middle Ages and through its long history has been the most important city of Provence.

IF YOU'RE JUST IN AVIGNON FOR THE DAY: Most of the public parking is located outside the city walls, south of the city, around the train station, as well as between the walls and the river on the west side of the city.

Mid Tarn Gorge (La Malène) to Arles
197 km / 122 mi

Avignon 183 km / 113 mi

Nîmes 182 km / 113 mi

DAY 13 EXPLORING PROVENCE

Michelin Regional Map # 527 (Provence-Alpes-Côte d'Azur)

Huge, historic, endlessly fascinating, Provence possesses a wealth of places to see, foods to savor, and "out-of-time" villages to explore..

LES BAUX-DE-PROVENCE(☆☆☆) (pop. 435) is an astonishing place, perched on a monumental spur of rock high above the surrounding country-side of vineyards, olive groves, and quarries. The mineral bauxite was discovered here in 1821. Half of Les Baux is composed of tiny climbing streets and ancient stone houses, inhabited for the most part by local craftspeople selling pottery, carvings, and assorted knickknacks. The other half, the "Ville Morte" (Dead Town), is a mass of medieval ruins, vestiges of Les Baux's glorious past when the town boasted 600 inhabitants and defensive impregna-bility. Parking is below the site at the entrance to the village.

Provence

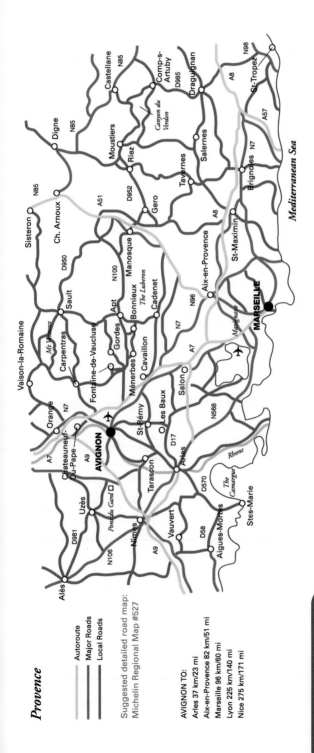

Autoroute
Major Roads
Local Roads

Suggested detailed road map:
Michelin Regional Map #527

AVIGNON TO:
Arles 37 km/23 mi
Aix-en-Provence 82 km/51 mi
Marseille 96 km/60 mi
Lyon 225 km/140 mi
Nice 275 km/171 mi

THE CAMARGUE(☆☆) has a nature reserve of 33,000 acres in which the native wildlife and wintering birds are protected. Here also are the famous wild horses and bulls. From the road you can see the pink flamingos. The principal town of La Camargue, Sainte-Maries-de-la-Mer, was painted by Van Gogh and is the venue of the famous gypsy pilgrimage that takes place every year on May 24 and 25. Very interesting, but if you go—hang on to your wallet and shy away from any five-year-olds who look like they're really playing an accordion. Papa isn't far behind. The town's main claim to fame is that of being a pilgrimage goal where, as legend has it, three Marys who were close to Jesus (reports disagree which three exactly) were set adrift in a boat from Palestine and washed up here. Relics of the group are in the fortress church.

GORDES(☆☆) (pop. 2,100) and the ABBEY of SÉNANQUE(☆☆)

An interesting hilltop village, Gordes is built in tiers on a rocky promontory. Four kilometers north on D 177 is the Abbey of Sénanque that was built by St. Bernard in 1148 and is one of the purest and best-preserved of France's Cistercian abbeys. Another intriguing nearby site is the Village de Bories(☆☆), which is now an outdoor museum of stone houses and rural life going back 500 years. You will find it three kilometers south of Gordes off the D 15.

ROUSSILLON(☆☆) (pop. 1,161) is named for the surrounding hills composed of 16 different shades of ochre rock, whose beauty is reflected in the stone houses. Follow the blue signs for parking and walk along the narrow Rue de l'Arcade to the cliff top where there is a view of the Vaucluse plateau and beyond the white limestone crest (it just looks like snow) of Mont Ventoux and the mountains of the Grand Luberon Range.

Other places of interest to consider include: Aigues-Mortes(★★★), St-Rémy(★), Vaison la Romaine(★★★), Orange(★★★), and Les Alpilles(★★).

DAY 14 PROVENCE TO MOUSTIERS-STE-MARIE

Michelin Regional Map # 527 (Provence-Alpes-Côte d'Azur)

From anywhere in the Avignon / Arles area, you need to follow the signs for the city of Apt. Road numbers will constantly be changing, so just follow the Apt signs until you connect with the N 100. About 12 km / 7 mi past the second exit to Cavaillon, and still on N 100, watch for the turnoff to Ménerbes. This is the Montagne du Luberon(★★★) region of Provence made famous around the world by the books of Peter Mayle, especially *A Year in Provence.* But much earlier, the beautiful hilltop village of Ménerbes(★) had already been discovered by painter Pablo Picasso and existentialist writer, Albert Camus.

From here make your way along the D 109 to Lacoste. The imposing castle ruins hovering over this hilltop village once belonged to that evil-doer, the Marquis de Sade.

Stay on the D 109 to Bonnieux(★), another village featured in the Mayle books. If you want to have a look around, park your car at the Place de la Liberté and follow the sign for the "Terrace" with views(☆) over the surrounding countryside.

As you leave Bonnieux, you will be on either D 3 or D 943 and again looking for signs that lead you to Apt. As you approach Apt, follow the signs for the N 100 (general direction: MANOSQUE / DIGNE.) At approximately 25 km / 16 mi after Apt, watch for the sign for Manosque on D 907. From Manosque, stay on D 907 following signs for Gréoux-les-Bains on D 82. From here your route will be via Riez and D 952 to your destination, Moustiers-Ste-Marie.

This little town(☆☆) (pop. 650) is situated dramatically at the base of towering rock formations near the entrance to the Grand Canyon du Verdon(☆☆☆). The famous pottery known as "Faience" was first produced here in 1697 and has a nice little museum located on the main street depicting the evolution of its wares down through the ages. The town has several small hotels plus the well-known (and super-expensive) Bastide de Moustiers, as well as a number of nice little restaurants.

150 km / 93 mi

DAY 15 MOUSTIERS TO THE CÔTE D'AZUR

Michelin Regional Map # 527 (Provence-Alpes-Côte d'Azur)

There are two routes through the Grand Canyon du Verdon. For the north side, follow signs "Canyon du Verdon" (general direction: CASTSELLANE). For the south side follow signs for the "Corniche Sublime" (general direction: COMPS-S-ARTUBY). The south route is more scenic, follows the canyon longer, and puts you further south toward the coast. Although a bit narrower in some places than the road on the north side, the south route is my personal favorite.

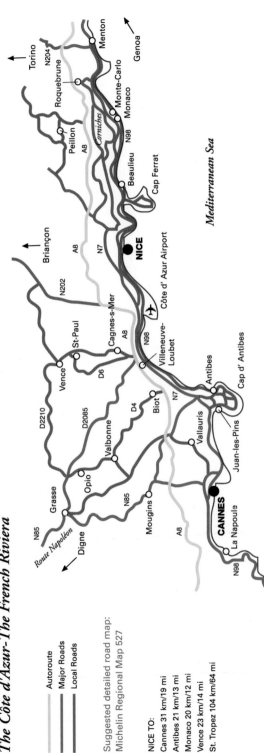

The Côte d'Azur–The French Riviera

Legend:
Autoroute
Major Roads
Local Roads

Suggested detailed road map:
Michelin Regional Map 527

NICE TO:
Cannes 31 km/19 mi
Antibes 21 km/13 mi
Monaco 20 km/12 mi
Vence 23 km/14 mi
St. Tropez 104 km/64 mi

After leaving the canyon from either of these routings, follow signs for Grasse and Nice.

155 km / 96 mi

If you had an early start this morning and took the Corniche Sublime, you may want to drive along one of the most beautiful parts of the Riviera coastal road to the area around Nice. From Comps, take D 955 to Draguignan, and follow signs to Fréjus and St-Raphaël. Pick up the N 7 through Fréjus to St-Raphaël following signs that will take you along the sea (Corniche l'Esterel) via Cap Roux, La Napoule, Cannes, Juan-les-Pins, Antibes, Nice, St-Jean-Cap-Ferrat, Monte-Carlo, and Menton. Take your pick.

210 km / 130 mi

An optional routing for those wanting to go straight to the Riviera in one day. This very basic route would take you from the Avignon area to Aix-en-Provence via the A 7 / A 8 autoroute (péage-toll.) The downside is you could end up spending a lot of time (and euros) on the autoroute. You also need to know that the sprawling city of Aix is difficult to navigate due to heavy and continuous traffic congestion that seems to be a way of life here, so that reaching the center usually takes lots of time and an inordinate amount of patience.

The ancient capital of Provence, Aix is best known for its stately main boulevard, the Cours Mirabeau, lined with majestic plane trees that overhang and envelop this unique thoroughfare. This is an old university city with a large and lively international student population that helps it to be the intellectual center of Provence. The old quarter known as Le Vieil Aix, with its myriad of narrow walking streets, is located just behind the Cours Mirabeau. Plenty of parking garages, but the nearest to the center is at the Place Charles de Gaulle.

From Aix go back to the autoroute A 8 (péage-toll) (general direction: NICE) and drive to Exit # 37 where you drop down to St-Raphaël and follow the N 98 coastal road via La Napoule and Cannes to Nice. Or if you're really in a hurry, stay on the A 8 all the way and pick your exit once on the Côte d'Azur. All are clearly marked from St-Tropez to the Italian border.

285 km / 177 mi

DAYS 16 & 17 ON THE RIVIERA

Michelin Regional Map # 527 (Provence-Alpes-Côte d"Azur)

The Côte d'Azur, also known as the French Riviera, extends along the Mediterranean coast from St-Raphaël to the Italian border at Menton and is one of the most favored spots on earth (just ask any billionaire Russian oligarch). The French traditionally take their vacations in July and August, and they come down here in droves. But it's not only the French that create the traffic; the driving situation is worsened by the influx of tourists from different countries all over Europe who bring with them their own unique blend of driving styles. Therefore, you need to drive defensively and carefully, especially within the numerous roundabouts which will come in all shapes and sizes.

BEST ADVICE: Do your best to avoid this area during July and August when it's packed. The rainiest months are October and November. Sunny winters are short and mild, but the best time to visit is in spring and fall. The region enjoys more or less Southern California-type weather.

Between Nice and Menton, near the Italian border, there are three famous roads at varying levels—the Lower, Middle, and Upper Corniches, each approximately 32 km / 20 mi in length.

≈ **The Lower Corniche** (Corniche Inférieure)(★★★), the coastal road, travels along the sea via Villefranche(★), Cap Ferrat(★★★), and Monte-Carlo(★★★). Very busy and heavily traveled this lower road offers lots to see and interesting stops.

≈ **The Middle Corniche** (Corniche Moyenne)(★★★), via Èze(★★★) and Beausoleil(★), takes the sea and coastal view up a notch, with mile after mile of dramatic scenery.

≈ **The Upper** (Grande Corniche(★★★), via La Turbie(★), Le Vistaëro(★★★), and Roquebrune(★), the highest and most spectacular of the three drives, was built by Napoleon along the original route of the Roman Via Julia Augusta, which dates from the 3rd century B.C. With stunning views of the coastline and sea at every turn, this road is not for the faint at heart. If you do plan to travel along this route, the recommendation is to drive it from east to west, i.e., Roquebrune to Nice. That way the driver becomes less distracted by the view—much to the relief of the passengers.

BEST ADVICE: Get a copy of the Michelin Green Guide *French Riviera* and choose a routing best suited to your interest and schedule.

CITIES, TOWNS, AND VILLAGES OF THE CÔTE D'AZUR

Nice(☆☆☆) (pop. metro area 890,000), known as "The Grand Dame" of the Riviera, was a village as early as 350 B.C. and probably a tribal center long before that, as prehistoric sites are still being uncovered in the vicinity. Ideally situated on the shores of a beautiful bay and framed by the awesome backdrop of the Alpes-Maritimes, Nice is a celebrated resort and the centerpiece of the entire Côte d'Azur. The palm-lined, flower-laden Promenade des Anglais is the most famous seaside boulevard in the world.

Èze(☆☆) (pop. 2,500) is a revealing example of the kind of nearly unapproachable site the ancient inhabitants of this area had to create to protect themselves in the days when the Saracens and pirates attacked them on a regular basis. The village is perched precariously around a pointed mass of rock 1300 feet above the sea just off the Middle Corniche. Parking is at the base of the rock.

Cap Ferrat(☆☆) (pop. 1,900), a peninsula jutting out into the Mediterranean, contains luxurious villas and gardens—most notably the Villa Ephrussi-de-Rothschild—with splendid views looking back to the coast and up at the not-too-distant Alps. Among the celebrities who once called this area home are writer Somerset Maugham, Charlie Chaplin, David Niven, and Edith Piaf.

Antibes(☆☆) (pop. 72,500) is an ancient Mediterranean fortified port town whose quiet charm is perhaps unequaled along the Côte d'Azur. Jutting out into the sea, Antibes contains a little harbor filled with pleasure yachts and fishing boats. On the ramparts stands the Château Grimaldi, now the Picasso Museum, housing one of the greatest Picasso collections in Europe.

Roquebrune(☆) (pop. 11,700) Located high above the coast on the Grande Corniche between Menton and Monaco, Roquebrune is an ancient fortress-village of narrow archways, twisting streets, and a ruined 10th century Carolingian castle, the oldest feudal citadel in France. The Donjon(☆) (Dungeon) is the main attraction here in what's left of the medieval stronghold that protected this part of the coast from those pesky Saracen raiders.

> **Le Donjon**
> Open daily – 10 am to 12:30 pm and 2 pm to 6:30 pm (Open till 7:30 pm Jul. and Aug.; Closes at 5 pm Nov. to Jan.)

St-Paul-de-Vence(☆☆) (pop. 2,900) can claim the title of the best-known of all the perched villages on the French Rivera. It was popularized in the 1920s when many noted artists lived there, occupying the little 16th century houses that flank the narrow, cobble-stoned streets. The feudal hamlet grew up on a bastion of rock, almost blending into it. Its ramparts overlook a peaceful setting of flowers and both olive and orange groves.

The star of this village is the famous rustic hotel-restaurant La Colombe d'Or. Located at the base of the village, it has to be considered a legend in its own time. In the thirties it was the happy and stimulating hangout of the likes of such artists as Picasso, Léger, Miro, Matisse, and Calder that resulted in the works of art that you see today on casual display throughout the premises. Later it became the favorite haunt of France's most celebrated movie two-some, Yves Montand and Simone Signoret. Still riding high today, La Colombe d'Or is guided by the venerable Roux family.

THE PRINCIPALITY OF MONACO

Monaco(☆☆☆) (pop. 32,000) is a sovereign state of some 500 acres consisting of the "old town" of Monaco and the "new town" of Monte-Carlo. There has been a customs union with France since 1865, the official language is French, and its currency is the euro. Non-French citizens pay no income tax (read: pop stars, Swedish tennis players, and European professional golfers.) Now then, who pays to keep the lights on and the tap water running, you may ask. Well, it's very interesting to see what gambling tables can do for an economy when organized crime is not involved.

The Monte-Carlo Casino is open daily from 12 noon. If you'd like to have an inside look, they offer a 40-minute tour. Men need a jacket and tie, and no one under 21 is admitted.

For the Palace (Palais du Prince) and the Ocean-ography Museum(☆☆) (workplace of Jacques Cousteau), follow signs up the hill to the large underground parking facility.

THE GREAT MODERN ART MUSEUMS

Musée Picasso (Antibes)
Open daily except Mon., Jun. to Sep. – 10 am to 6 pm (Open till 8 pm Wed. and Fri.); Oct. to May – 10 am to 12 noon and 2 pm to 6 pm. Closed Jan. 1, May 1, Nov. 1, and Dec. 25.

Matisse Chapel
(Chapelle de Rosaire-Vence)
Open Tue. and Thu. – 10 am to 11:30 am and 2 pm to 5:30 pm.; Mon., Wed., Sat. – 2 pm to 5:30 pm.; Sun. 10 am for Mass. Closed mid Nov. to mid Dec.

Maeght Foundation
(Northwest of St-Paul de Vence)
Open daily Jul. 1 to Sep. 30 – 10 am to 7 pm; Oct. 1 to Jun. 30 – 10 am to 12:30 pm and 2:30 pm to 6 pm.

Musée Fernand-Léger (Biot)

Open daily except Tue., Jul. 1. to Sep. 30. – 10:30 am to 6 pm; Oct. 1 to Jun. 30 – 10 am to 12:30 pm and 2 pm to 5:30 pm. Closed Jan. 1, May 1, and Dec. 25.

Musée Renoir (Cagnes-sur-Mer)

This small and intimate house is where August Renoir spent the last 12 years of his long life—painting up to the very end. On the first floor are his two studios, preserved just as they were during his lifetime. This museum feels a bit like Monet's house in Giverny, but is much more personal and not nearly as crowded. The 19th century house is surrounded by a beautiful garden, filled with lemon, orange, and olive trees. If you like the French Impressionist Art movement, this place could provide you with some very fond memories.

Open daily except Tue. – 10 am to noon and 2 pm to 6 pm. (Closes at 5 pm Oct. to Apr.)

NOTE: You will find an English language radio at 106.5 FM, with news, music, local events, and traffic information serving the English-speaking communities from St-Tropez to Menton.

DAY 18 CÔTE D'AZUR TO GAP

Michelin Regional Map # 527 (Provence-Alpes-Côte d'Azur) and # 523 (Rhone-Alpes)

Say goodbye to the Côte d'Azur this morning, departing via the Route Napoléon(☆), which begins in the town of Golfe-Juan, the next town west of Juan-les-Pins. Watch for the signs reading Route Napoléon that will take you to the N 7 leading to the N 85.

As the name implies, this was the route taken by Napoleon as he marched his ragtag but still loyal troops to Paris to reclaim his emperor's crown after his escape from the island of Elba in March of 1815. This well-traveled route also featured Hannibal of Carthage herding his elephants across the Alps in 219 B.C. en route to do battle with Rome. He made it—the elephants didn't.

Drive via Grasse (pop. 44,000) Since the 19th century, Grasse (☆☆) has been the world's perfume capital, set in the midst of jasmine and roses. One of the best-known perfume factories is the Fragonard Parfumerie, named after the French painter of the 18th century. Also of interest is the Museum of Perfumery, displaying bottles and vases that trace the industry back to ancient times.

From Grasse, remain on the Route Napoléon and follow signs for Castellane / Digne. You will travel via Sisteron, with its amazing views(☆☆) from the *Citadelle* overlooking the surrounding countryside, to Gap. Overnight could be in either of the towns, but Gap has a population of 36,000, while Sisteron has only 7,000. There are several small towns and villages just north of Gap, but advance reservations (or early arrival) are recommended during the high season.

Need to make up some time? The autoroute A 51 runs parallel to the N 85 nearly all the way from Sisteron to Gap.

> Nice to Gap 260 km / 161 mi
>
> Nice to Sisteron 205 km / 127 mi

DAY 19 SISTERON / GAP
TO THE BEAUJOLAIS WINE REGION

Michelin Regional Map # 519 (Bourgogne)

Today's route stays on N 85 toward Grenoble. As you approach the city, follow the blue autoroute signs for Lyon via the A 48. Since our destination is the Beaujolais area just north of Lyon, we think it best to utilize the autoroute system to quickly get you around the metropolitan area of France's third largest city. Don't forget about rush hour, as well as Sunday late afternoon traffic.

As you approach Lyon, stay on the autoroute following the blue signs (general direction: MACON /PARIS) on A 46. Leave the autoroute at Exit # 30

leading to Belleville. Here you are at the entrance of the beautiful (and bountiful) Beaujolais wine country. For both food and wine this is an area steeped in culinary tradition since Roman times. You will find accommodations here in the small villages along the wine routes in the countryside—but plan ahead.

Gap to Belleville 290 km / 180 mi

Sisteron to Belleville 345 km / 213 mi

POSSIBLE SIDE TRIP

If you have the time to give the city of Lyon a closer look than most tourists do, you won't be disappointed. Here are a few facts about this remarkable city—just in case.

Lyon(☆☆☆), the third largest city in France (pop. 1.4 million), started life in 100 B.C. as the Roman town of Lugdunum and was the birthplace of Roman emperors Claudius and Caracalla. However it was to the silk industry that Lyon owed its great riches and reputation. From the breeding of the silk worm to weaving and dyeing, Lyon carried on a world-wide trade that featured goods ranging from simple silks and velvets to the most expensive damasks and brocades.

Gypsies on the Route du Vin selling wares
– keep moving

The Place Bellecour in the center of the La Presqu'ile district is the lively heart of this bustling city, and here you will find restaurants and hotels in all categories. Public parking is available here as well as at the nearby Place Carnot at the end of the walking street (rue Victor Hugo) and behind the Perrache rail and bus station complex.

However, on the other side of the river from the Place Bellecour is the old town, known as the Vieux Lyon, with many fine Renaissance mansions plus a sprinkling of late Gothic houses. This area is great for exploring its medieval streets on foot to gain a close-up look at its unique covered passages (*traboules*) and inner courtyards.

Oh yes, the city is also a gourmand's delight, as some of the finest and best-known restaurants in France are located here, including the nearby culinary three-star shrine of Paul Bocuse at Collonges-au-Mont-d'Or. And that's only the start. Pound for pound, the best single area for gastronomic excellence in France is to be found in Lyon.

NOTE: The TGV high-speed trains operate from both Part Dieu and Perrache train stations, and all major self-drive companies have locations at both stations.

DAY 20 VIA THE ROUTE DE BEAUJOLAIS TO BEAUNE

Michelin Regional Map # 519 (Bourgogne)

Make your way through this unique wine-growing area of green rolling hills and old villages where life hasn't changed very much down through the years. The Route de Beaujolais (mostly along the D 68) takes you north via the celebrated wine villages of Villie-Morgon, Fleurie, Chenas, Juliénas, and St-Amour.

Many travelers choose to spend another night in this bucolic countryside. For those of you who do not, it's on to Cluny to see what's left of one of France's most famous abbeys as you make your way to Beaune.

Keep working your way north towards Pouilly-Fuissé, where signs will connect you with the N 79. Follow the signs to Cluny. Once in town, you will find signs directing you to the ruins of the ancient Abbaye de Cluny(★★).

This famous abbey, from which sprung 200 monasteries and convents, was the devotional center of Christendom in the 11th and 12th centuries and the rival of Rome itself. Of its great Romanesque church, the largest and most powerful church complex in the Christian world before the construction of St. Peter's in Rome, there remains only a wing of the transept and a few chapels of what once was. A sad, but impressive site.

Abbaye de Cluny
Open daily Jul., Aug., and Sep. – 9 am to 7 pm (Closes at 6 pm in Sep.); Apr., May, and Jun. – 9:30 am to 12 noon and 2 pm to 6 pm; Oct. – 9:30 am to 12 noon and 2 pm to 5 pm; Nov. to Mar. – 10 am to 12 noon and 2 pm to 4 pm. Closed Jan. 1, May 1, and Dec. 25.

Though it's usually passed by, the town of Cluny(☆) (pop. 4,400) itself has a number of medieval and Renaissance buildings including some unique old houses built in Romanesque style that are worth a look.

From Cluny you can drive north on D 981 via Cormatin, Buxy, Givry, and Chagny to Beaune, the wine capital of Burgundy.

The pleasant and charming French provincial town of Beaune (☆☆) (pop. 22,000) was originally the 14th century residence of the Dukes of Burgundy and is still surrounded by defensive walls—now frequently occupied by wine cellars. In this capital of one of the world's greatest wine regions, the grape is Beaune's raison d'être, and for the wine lover, this town has everything, including the best wine museum in France. Housed in a 15th century building, the Musée du Vin de Bourgogne(☆☆) traces the entire history of winemaking.

The main historic attraction here is the ancient hospital known by the dual name Hôtel-Dieu(☆☆☆) and Hospice de Beaune. Perfectly preserved from the Middle Ages, the hospital was built in 1443 by Nicolas Rolin, Chancellor of the Duke of Burgundy. After the Hundreds Years' War, Beaune was devastated and devoid of basic supplies. To redeem the situation the Chancellor and his wife decided to found a "Hospice for the Poor." They endowed it with an annual income (a salt works) plus its own resources (vineyards) that provide its income to this very day.

From the Middle Ages to the 20th century, countless sick were taken in and cared for by the Sisters of the Hospice de Beaune. In 1971 its medical activities were transferred to a modern hospital, but the adjacent retirement home was retained. Today the Hospice owns and operate 150 acres of prime vineyards, and each year since 1859 have organized the most famous wine auction in the world. Definitely a "must see."

150 km / 93 mi

DAY 21 EXPLORING THE VINEYARDS OF BURGUNDY

Michelin Regional Map # 519 (Bourgogne)

The wine districts of Beaune are known as the Côte d'Or (the Golden Hillside) that stretches for some 30 miles from just south of Dijon at the village of Fixin in the north to the village of Santenay in the south.

The northern half of the Côte d'Or is called the Côte de Nuit and produces the famous red wines of the Pinot Noir grape. The best-known vineyards in this district include Gevrey-Chambertin, La Tâche, Chambolle-Musigny, Vougeot, and Romanée-Conti.

The southern half of the Côte d'Or is the Côte de Beaune, where the grandest white wine in the world is produced using the Chardonnay grape. The best-known vineyards here are Puligny-Montrachet and Meursault.

There are lots of opportunities in this region for tastings in wine cellars as well as the great wine estates such as the Château de Meursault and Clos Vougeot. However if you're looking for a smaller more intimate setting, watch for the signs reading Dégustation / Vente (wine tasting / sales). Don't forget, the whole idea is to sell their wine.

The most interesting place I know of in the whole of Burgundy is a house in the middle of the village of Puligny-Montrachet called La Table d'Olivier Leflaive. Usually presided over by Olivier himself, the wine tastings feature a famous wine from a tiny, but famous village familiar to connoisseurs the world over.

BEST ADVICE: One of the best ways to do some regional wine tasting is to pay a visit to the **Marché aux Vins**, located in the center of Beaune near the tourist office at rue Nicholas Rolin. This memorable experience takes place in a medieval building, parts of which date back to the 13th century. For a nominal entry charge you can sample the great reds of Clos de Vougeot and Vosne Romanée and the great whites of Puligny-Montrachet and Meursault. Armed with your personal sommelier's wine tasting cup (included in the entrance fee), you make your own way through 16 individual tasting stations (each with their own spittoon) placed at candle-lit intervals through these ancient wine storage tunnels.

All in all, a singular experience, and it's even better if you're staying in Beaune itself, so you can just walk, not drive, back to your hotel.

> **Marché aux Vins**
> Open daily from 9:30 am to 12 noon and from 2:30 pm to 6:30 pm.

DAY 22 BEAUNE TO FONTAINEBLEU / BARBIZON

Michelin Regional Maps # 514 (Ile-de-France)

From the ring road that encircles Beaune in a counterclockwise direction, follow the exit signs reading Pommard/Volney on D 973 leading to La Rochepot.

Here is an interesting little feudal castle() dating from the 15th century and now faithfully restored.

If you have the time, it's worth a visit

> **La Rochepot**
> Open daily except Tue., Apr. to Jun. – 10 am to 11 am and 2 pm to 5:30 pm; Jul. and Aug. 10 am to 12 noon and 2 pm to 6 pm; Sep. and Oct. – 10 am to 11:30 am and 2 pm to 6:30 pm. Closed the rest of the year.

Continue following signs for Arnay-le-Duc and Sau-lieu on N 6 to Avallon. In Avallon follow signs for Vézelay via the Valée du Cousin.

The beautiful tiny hilltop village of Vézelay (pop. 500) was originally settled by the Celts in the 9th century and is dominated by the historic Basillique Ste-Madeleine, said to contain the bones of Mary Magdalene, making it one of the great treasures of Burgundy and France. In the basilica, the marvelous tympanum (portal sculpture) of the central doorway and the 12 columns in the vast nave are world-renowned and have been featured in art and architecture publications for decades.

In the 11th and 12th centuries, Vézelay was one of the most important places of pilgrimage in the Christian world. It was from here in 1146 St. Bernard preached the call for the second Crusade in the presence of King Louis VII. It remains to this day one of France's most distinguished sights.

Parking is at the base of the village.

After your visit, follow the sign for Auxerre. If time is a factor, you may wish to pick up the A 6 autoroute to speed you on your way to the Fontainebleu area.

BEAUNE TO FONTAINEBLEAU / BARBIZON

The sign out of Vézelay for Auxerre will lead you to the A 6 autoroute (péage-toll) entrance just north of Avallon near Nitry. The use of the autoroute will cut the driving time in half. Approximately 84 km / 52 mi past Auxerre, take Exit # 15 leading to the N 7 to Fontainebleau. At the roundabout, follow the château sign.

Even more than Versailles, Fontainebleau is the palace most closely linked with the history of France. Nearly all French sovereigns, from Louis VII to Napoleon, were fond of Fontainebleau(★★★), and this very fondness was the cause of innumerable alterations. Those who chiefly left their mark upon it were François I, who began the building of the palace on the site of an ancient hunting lodge created by Capetian kings in the 12th century; Louis XIV, for the gardens designed by Le Notre; and Napoleon and Josephine, who changed a great deal of the interior to suit their own tastes and whose private apartments can be visited.

Fontainebleau
Open daily except Tue.- 9:30 am to 6 pm; Oct. to May closes at 5 pm. Closed Jan.1 and Dec. 25. Last admission 45 minutes before closing.

BEST ADVICE: You've had a long and busy day, and although you're close to Paris (65 km / 40 mi) the best idea (if time permits) is to forget about struggling through Paris rush-hour traffic and stay in Fontainebleau (pop. 16,000) itself—or better yet, in the nearby famous artist's village of Barbizon for a leisurely "last night on the road" dinner and overnight.

Barbizon(☆☆) (pop. 1,600) is located just off N 7, 10 km / 6 mi north of Fontainebleau.

Here is the small and cozy single street village that became famous because of the pre-Impressionist landscape artists who worked here using nature as their subject. Led by Theodore Rousseau (1812-1867), this style came to be known as the "Barbizon School." The tiny hotel where many of them lived is now a museum, including works of Corot, Courbet, Daubigny, Millet, and Rousseau.

Robert Louis Stevenson once lived here in the house that is now one of the best-known hotel-restaurants in France, the Hôtellerie du Bas-Bréau, run lovingly by the family of Jean-Pierre Fava for the past three generations. A definite splurge, but worth every euro.

Want something easier on the pocket book? Try the Auberge les Alouttes.

285 km / 177 mi

DAY 23 FONTAINEBLEU / BARBIZON TO PARIS

Michelin Regional Map # 514 (Ile-de-France)

Signs will lead you to the A 6 autoroute (péage-toll) for Paris. As you approach the city and the périphérique, follow signs for the neighborhood you need to reach:

FONTAINEBLEAU / BARBIZON TO PARIS

FOR CENTRAL PARIS: Arc d'Triomphe, Champs Élysées, Place de la Concorde, and Louvre.

Follow the sign Périphérique Ouest (west) and take this ring road all the way to the exit for Pte. Maillot. Circle around to the left in the roundabout and turn right just past the blue glass building. The Arc de Triomphe (Étoile) and the Champs Élysées are straight ahead. As you approach the Arc and see all those cars circling around, just remember that the vehicles ON THE RIGHT have the right of way and that's what makes it work. Make your way slowly counterclockwise, playing a little give and take as you ease your way around. Geographically, you entered the Étoile at 6 o'clock and you want to exit at 12 o'clock. At 3 o'clock start making your way, bearing right towards 12 o'clock and, voila! Down the Champs Élysées you go and into the Place de la Concorde.

FOR THE LEFT BANK: St-Germain-des-Prés, Latin Quarter, Montparnasse, Place St-Michel, and Luxemborg Gardens.

Look for the sign indicating Périphérique Ouest (west), keeping to the right and following the sign and right turn exit into the Pte. d'Orléans. Keep straight. You are now on the Avenue du Général du Clerc. See that big **church** ahead of you where the street splits? Bear to the **right** of the church and stay on this main street that will lead you to right into to the Place-St-Michel. If you're heading for Montparnasse, bear **left** at the church into Avenue du Maine.

FOR PARIS NORTH: Montmartre and Sacré-Coeur as well as the train stations Gare du Nord and the Gare de l'Est.

Follow signs for Périphérique Ouest (west) and exit at the Pte. de Clignacourt. For the Gare St-Lazare train stations exit at Pte. St-Ouen.

FOR PARIS EAST: Bastille, Gare de Lyon, Pompidou Centre, Place des Vosges, and Le Marais.

Follow signs for Périphérique Est (east) and exit at the Pte. de Vincennes.

Once you're in your "area," white signs will direct you to the various neighborhoods, e.g., Opéra, Louvre, Bastille, Montmartre, Bois de Boulogne, Invalides, etc.

BEST ADVICE: For a really good map to help you get into Paris, as well as for use after you've settled in, the Michelin *Paris Tourism Map # 7* can't be beat! Just the right size and contains all kinds of useful information.

FOR AIRPORT CHARLES DE GAULLE (CDG): (Aéroport Roissy – Charles de Gaulle) – 26 km / 16 mi northeast of Paris.

From the Fontainebleau / Barbizon area, take the A 6 autoroute toward Paris. As you approach the city, follow signs Périphérique Est (east) and blue signs reading Lille / Bruxelles / Charles de Gaulle with the jet logo. Follow signs for **Car Rental Return** (or simply Car Rental); in French the sign reads **Location de Voitures.**

BEST ADVICE: You need to know exactly which terminal (aréogare) your flight leaves from **before** you arrive at the airport complex.

THERE ARE THREE TERMINALS (AEROGARE) AT CDG:

Aérogare 1. International flights including United, Lufthansa, and SAS

Aérogare 2. Actually six separate "halls" (departure points)

- **2 A** Air France, Air Canada, American, Continental, El Al, and US Airways

- **2 B** Air France, British Airways, Swiss Airlines

- **2 C** Air France, Aeroflot

- **2 D** Air France, Austrian, Finnair, Iberia

- **2 E** Air France to USA (LAX, MIA, JFK, PHL, SFO, SEA, IAD). Delta and Northwest to USA.

- **2 F** Air France, Alitalia, KLM, JAL, and Middle East Airlines (Beirut)

Aérogare 3. Charter flights and low-cost carriers - easyJet, Zoom (Canada), and Air Berlin.

NOTE: Two additional terminals are currently being built at CDG with more on the way. Changes for airline departure points are bound to change.

FOR ORLY AIRPORT (ORY)

14 km / 9 mi southwest of Paris

Approximately 45 km / 28 mi north of Fontainebleau on the A 6, exit signs will lead you directly into the airport complex. Follow signs for **Rental Car Return** (or simply Car Return); in French the sign reads **Location de Voitures.**

THERE ARE TWO TERMINALS **(ÁEROGARE)** AT ORY

- Orly Sud (south) - easyJet, El Al, and Swiss Airlines

- Orly Ouest (west)- Air France, Iberia, and TAP Portugal

NOTE: For those avoiding the autoroute, follow the green signs for the N 7 that runs parallel to the autoroute all the way into Paris to the Pte. d'Italie. As you approach the Porte d'Italie, follow the sign for the entrance to the périphérique. You want either Ouest (west) or Est (east). See above for destinations reached from the périphérique.

From Fontainebleau / Barbizon to:

Paris (Notre-Dame) – 65 km / 40 mi

Orly Airport – 55 km / 35 mi

Charles de Gaulle Airport – 90 km / 56 mi

INFORMATIONAL ROAD SIGNS

Driving forbidden

No Entry

No entry for cars or motorbikes

No parking or stopping

No parking

No left turn

No U turn

No passing by cars

Mandatory direction

Drive this side

Maximum speed limit

End of speed limit

Minimum speed limit

End of passing prohibition

End of prohibition

Yield

You do not have right of way

Roadway with priority

End of roadway with priority

Main roadway with priorty

Junction with priority to the right

Dangerous curve

Dangerous bend

Uneven surface

Narrowing roadway

Unguarded pier - danger

Crosswalk

Children present

Railway crossing with barriers

Rail crossing without barriers

Other dangers

Hospital - ER

Stop - Police

Stop - Customs

Stop - Toll

Priority over opposite direction

Priority given to traffic from the opposite direction

Two-way traffic

Tourist information

School bus

One way

Road works

Detour

Take your ticket for the péage

International road sign Designation

Rest stop plazas plus distance to next two

Pay toll at
1000 meters

Peage atten-
dant cash or
credit

Pay by
credit card

Automatic
pay with
euro coins

Dead end

Parking

Meter park-
ing

Begin auto
route

End auto-
route

Roundabout

Alternate
route

Countdown
markers

How to drive the roundabout

**White painted squares on the pavement means yield to
vehicles within the roundabout**

FRANCE INDEX OF PLACE NAMES

INTERNATIONAL DRIVER'S LICENSE

This document is correctly called an International Driver's Permit. It **is not** a license at all, but a piece of paper used only to help police translate your valid state- or province-issued driver's license. Rental car companies do not require this "document," but if you think you want one, buy **only** from the American Automobile Association. Cost—about $10. Beware of online providers.

CAR RENTAL INSURANCE

In addition to the normal coverage, it is always advisable to have the CDW (Collision Damage Waiver) that provides a zero deductible in the event of an accident or a nasty bump in your fender. Some credit card companies advertise that they include CDW or LDW (theft) coverage; however, it's imperative to check with them to see **exactly** what coverage they actually provide. The supplemental insurance is not cheap, but it does eliminate what could be a hassle-filled situation when you return the vehicle.

BEST ADVICE: Have a discussion with your hometown insurance provider to go over the CDW. It is also important to review the coverage provided overseas by your homeowner's **and** health insurance policies. For instance, Medicare will not help you in Europe. Group policies will usually cover partial costs. You need to have all the facts—essential in the "peace of mind" department.

I'm interested in your comments, opinions, and suggestions. Email me at:
orv@autoventure.com

or write to me at:
Orv Strandoo
720 Third Ave, Suite 2200,
Seattle, WA 98104

NOTES

NOTES

_____
_____
_____
_____
_____
_____
_____
_____
_____
_____
_____
_____
_____
_____
_____
_____
_____
_____
_____
_____
_____
_____
_____
_____
_____
_____
_____
_____

NOTES

_____
_____
_____
_____
_____
_____
_____
_____
_____
_____
_____
_____
_____
_____
_____
_____
_____
_____
_____
_____
_____
_____
_____
_____
_____
_____

NOTES

_____

_____

_____

_____

_____

_____

_____

_____

_____

_____

_____

_____

_____

_____

_____

_____

_____

_____

_____

_____

_____

_____

_____

_____

_____

_____

_____